Journey to E

A Handbook for Walla Walla Valley,

& Northern Idaho Wineries

(and a few places to eat and sleep)

By

Dave Westfall

Sam Lange

Vineyard Sky

By Alexei Kazantsev

Copyright @ 2009 Dave Westfall
All rights reserved

ISBN 978-0-9819957-0-0

Credits

Cover Inspiration by Cari Westfall

Book cover created by Mike Bold, Digital Itch

Stickmen revision by Pat McVay

Vineyard Photographs by Alexei Kazantsev

14th Street Publishing
Spokane, WA 99204

First Edition

Acknowledgements

We would like to thank those people who have been particularly helpful in our own journey.

Our editor C. Lee Sage has tried to keep us on course by disputing facts that we made up, suggesting we try not to consume a wine from every winery each time we sit down to put our thoughts on paper and to give us encouragement when our minds got stuck in fermentation, she said it was the "yeast of our problems." We thank her for her guidance and if she is reading this, we would like a forwarding address.

Dedication –For us it starts with our departed friend, Bob Jones, who every Monday at chemo would talk about the good old days when wine and food was a passion (and perhaps a story or two from the Scotch Malt Liquor Society). Bob and Dave catered many dinners together, taught wine classes for more than twenty years and every super bowl Sunday had a "hot off" with Bob's eggplant from hell usually winning first prize. Bob encouraged this project and we are sure he is waiting in line for the first complimentary copy so he can share it with the Great Grape-maker.

Dave--Lou Anne Moxcey and Rick Sorenson have been life long friends and were cohorts at the Spokane Wine Company. My partners in the winery, David Page, John Mueller and Michael Manz (1948-2006) have all contributed to the spirit of the book. My great niece, Cari Westfall, helped design the book cover and my son, David, says "Don't forget the next generation." And to my sister, Denise, and my Harvard critic, David Jost, who both said, "Never give up, someone will eventually get one of your jokes" I say, "Have you heard this one? A grape went into a bar and started to whine …"

Sam –My wife, Tonya, who encouraged Dave and me to find a good delivery pizza place at three in the morning because she wasn't going to make us Carnegie Deli style pastrami sandwiches or a baked chicken with Chartres Street jambalaya. (You have to love K-Paul's). And of course, to my brother in kilts, Gary Laing who started this journey with me back in 1984 at the Grape and Grain.

About this book:

Because the wine industry is constantly changing we have tried to figure out how to update this book on an hourly basis. Our editor, C. Lee Sage, tells us this is impossible and we have to admit our failure. So, our goal is to give you the current information as we see it, add a few comments about particular wineries and restaurants and then let the grapes fall where they may. As we get responses from readers we will update our information and by the 214th edition we hope to be fairly complete. If we left out your favorite restaurant, let us know – we want to try it; if we left out a winery or one has closed, let us know; if you have any additional complaints, contact Sam.

Dave tells Sam that they forgot a winery in Walla Walla.

Table of Contents

	Introduction	vi
	Timeline	viii

Walla Walla

	Wineries	1
Part I	Wine Tour	4
Part II	Geek Wine Tour	12
Part III	Cemetery	53
Part IV	Vineyards	55
Part V	Gotta Eat – lunch or dinner	62
	Special Occasions	67
	Coffee and Dessert	68
	Outside Walla Walla	70
Part VI	Ain't Gonna Eat There No More	72
Part VII	Gotta Sleep Walla Walla	74
Part VIII	Walla Walla Links	76

Spokane & Northern Idaho

	Wineries	77
Part I	Wine Tour	78
Part II	Geek Wine Tour	84
Part III	Cemetery	94
Part IV	Gotta Eat – Breakfast	96
	lunch or dinner	100
Part V	Food Cemetery	124
Part VI	Gotta Sleep Spokane	126
Part VII	Gotta Eat Coeur d'Alene	128
Part VIII	Gotta Eat Lewiston-Sandpoint	136
Part IX	Gotta Sleep Coeur d'Alene	140
Part X	Spokane Links	142
	Author Biographies	143
	Glossary	144

Introduction:

When I made a left turn off Silverado Trail to go visit Charles Wagner at Caymus in 1978 I didn't realize I was about to change my passion for wine into a career in the wine industry. After an hour lecture from Charlie about prohibition, sacramental wine and the history of the California wine industry I asked why he was so enthusiastic about the wine industry after all these years. He told me that he was lucky enough to have seen the changes and if I paid attention to where I came from I would see some changes too. That conversation led to emphasizing wine/food pairing in my catering business and opening a wine store in 1984 (down the street Sam was in the process of opening his own retail wine store); in 1987 I started a fine wine distributorship and finally, in 1997, taking the grape juice plunge, I crushed my first grapes at Grande Ronde Cellars.

In less than three decades the Washington Wine Industry has grown from nineteen wineries in 1980 to more than six hundred wineries in 2009; from less than one million gallons of wine in 1978 to more than twenty million gallons of wine in 2006. Washington currently ranks second in total wine production in the United States with more than one hundred twenty-seven tons produced in 2007.

Producing more red grapes than white grapes (57 to 43 percent) the Washington Wine industry emphasizes premium wines. Washington's growing season averages more than seventeen hours of summer daylight per day – two more than California's prime growing regions. There are currently eleven American Viticulture Areas (AVA) in Washington State: Yakima (1983); Walla Walla Valley (1984); Columbia Valley (1984); Puget Sound (1995); Red Mountain (2001); Columbia Gorge (2004); Horse Heaven Hills (2005); Wahluke Slope (2006); Rattlesnake Hills (2006); Snipes Mountain (2009) and Lake Chelan (2009). Ancient Lakes is currently seeking AVA status as well.

Our conclusion is that even the most experienced wine tasters can't visit all 600 plus wineries in one weekend. (Sam and I have tried.) That's why we have developed a series of books intended for those who want to visit wineries in a specific area. We will look at each wine region as if you are on a food and wine tour. We'll give you current information on wineries. (Although we found this to be a far more difficult task than we had assumed it would be. Some of the wineries seem to exist only on paper.) Some of the bonded wineries have produced little or no wine. Sometimes a winery was bonded under one name and because of various reasons wound up using a different name to produce the wine. (Two examples are Covey Run which started out as Quail Run but was forced to change its name and Lone Canary which started out as Wild Canary and changed its name before the first wine was produced.). Despite calls, emails and voodoo grape rituals we weren't able to get information directly from all of the wineries so we used our internet detective skills to gather clues about their wine establishments. I'm sure we will get a few calls after the book comes out and we apologize in advance if we left anything, or anyone, out but we do believe that at the time of publication the information that is in the book is accurate (within a glass or two of wine at least). The restaurants are all places we have eaten at, or they have been recommended to us by more than one of the local wineries. The hotels are there for your convenience. Because this information changes rapidly we have included websites for your convenience. We hope you enjoy this book and all of the books in our series.

Stain glass portrait of Dave by Richard Westfall

Timeline

4 billion years ago	Earth formed.
80 million years ago	Cascade Mountains formed so there would be a dry side for grapes.
34 million years ago	Creation of Columbia Plateau and lava flows create ground for future vineyards.
40 thousand years ago	First ash deposits of Mt. St. Helens. Potters sell urns to put wine in, before the invention of the bottle.
10 thousand years ago	The Washington ice age. (No relation to the state or ice wines – just a really cold time in Eastern Washington). First vineyard manager, Kennewick Man, sets up house in Tri-cities.
1792	Robert Gray names Columbia River after his ship. Applies for first AVA but the Queen rejects application. Instead she sets up a Bureau of Tobacco, Rum and Muskets. It takes one hundred and ninety-two years to get the first AVA approved. (Author's note: This is referred to as the Stomp Act.)
1807	David Thompson charts Columbia River and presumably cuts out sites for future vineyards. (Ever heard of Thompson seedless?)
1825	First grapes cultivated in Washington State by Hudson Bay Company near Fort Vancouver.

1853	Washington Territory created. Native Americans insist it was already there.
1858	John Mullan began construction of the Mullan road from Walla Walla to Fort Benton. He completed the wagon trail in 1862. The authors also took five years to complete their first book in the "Journey to …" series. Like Mullan we ran into a few obstacles during our journey.
1889	Washington becomes 42nd state. The citizens of Spokane Falls celebrate by burning most of the downtown area.
1974	World's Fair in Spokane.
1978	Leonetti is first winery in Walla Walla.
1980	Worden's is first winery in Spokane.
1984	Walla Walla Valley becomes an AVA.
2004	Dave begins work on book. Kim Clothier of L'Ecole tells Dave it will be hard to include all fifty wineries in Walla Walla. In 2008 Dave realizes that by procrastinating there are now a hundred bonded wineries in Walla Walla and twenty in Spokane and Northern Idaho.
2009	Dave and Sam finish first edition of "Journey to…" series. Sam tells everyone that it didn't really take that much time and he is confident the next book will take less than four billion years.

Walla Walla Wineries, Vineyards,

Restaurants and Hotels

The Walla Walla Valley is located in the southeast corner of Washington State. Washington wineries in this area have been touted by wine writers and publications throughout the world. For thirty years Walla Walla wines have been receiving praise from publications like the *Wine Spectator* and *Wine Advocate*. The Cabernet Sauvignons, Syrahs and Merlots have been ranked in the top 100 by *Wine Spectator* and can be found throughout the United States. The wines have received 90 plus ratings annually from *The Wine Advocate* and *Wine Enthusiast*. The Walla Walla Valley appellation includes 530 square miles of land from the southeast corner of Washington State to the northeast tip of Oregon. This region lies within the larger Columbia Valley appellation. Vineyard acreage has increased from less than 100 acres in 1980 to 800 acres in 1999 to 1600 acres in 2008.

History of Walla Walla

Native Americans named the region Walla Walla, meaning "many waters." The first cultivated grapevines in the Walla Walla Valley area can be traced to the late 1850s. French fur traders made wine for personal consumption and later, as the production increased, for commercial purposes at the beginning of the 20th century. Most vineyards were abandoned during prohibition which all but squashed the idea of a wine industry in the Walla Walla Valley area.

In 1977 the first post-prohibition commercial winery was established in Walla Walla and just seven years later the region was federally recognized as a "unique American Viticultural Area" (AVA). It was the third Washington State AVA designation. In 1983 Walla Walla was home to three wineries and less than 100 acres of vineyards. Today there are more than 100 bonded wineries and over 1600 acres of grapes in the area.

The days are long and hot, the evenings cool. This temperature variation allows the grapes to develop flavor and natural acidity. The soils are a combination of loam, silt, loess and cobbles which were deposited thousands of years ago. The growers also have the opportunity to control the amount of water a plant receives through irrigation.

The region is known for its red grapes, particularly Merlot, Cabernet Sauvignon and Syrah. Several vineyards are experimenting with Cabernet Franc, Malbec, Grenache, Tempranillo, Barbera, Nebbiolo, Sangiovese and Grand Vidure (Carmenere). There are also some plantings of white wine grapes; most notably: Chardonnay, Sauvignon Blanc, Gewurztraminer, Semillon, Pinot Gris, Riesling and Viognier.

National and International Recognition

Wines from the Walla Walla Valley have earned recognition from *Bon Appétit*, *Decanter*, *Gourmet*, *Sunset*, the *Wall Street Journal*, *Wine Advocate*, *Wine Enthusiast*, *Wine Spectator* and *Wine and Spirits* magazines.

Annual Events

Walla Walla

May

The first two weekends in May include spring release events and the Balloon Stampede.

November

The first weekend in November is the fall release for many of the wineries.

December

The first weekend in December is the Holiday Barrel weekend.

Spokane

Mother's Day Weekend and the Weekend before Thanksgiving are traditionally the Spring and Fall release parties for all of the Spokane wineries.

Part I

The Wine Tour vs. Geek Tour

We have divided the Walla Walla winery section into two parts. The first part we call the Wine Tour. These are wineries that are open most of the year. (Note: many wineries close for a few weeks after the first of the year, or have reduced hours. Some wineries are just open over special weekends and others we call "phantom of the bonderas" don't seem to be open at all.) The wineries we put in the Wine Tour area are there for first time visitors with a limited amount of time. We think these wineries will usually be open (either daily or on the weekends) and each of them have a lot to offer in terms of tasting room, grounds, wines that are actually made from Walla Walla Valley grapes, people who are part of the history of the area, etc.

The second group of wineries is the Wine Geek Tour. These are all of the other wineries. As geeks we find their stories compelling, even the ones we don't know. (You might note that the great-grandparent of all the Walla Walla wineries, Leonetti, is in this section as are some other "noted" wineries. These wineries are open on such a limited basis you most likely will be unable to visit them on your tour.)

This system isn't perfect and we expect that some of the wineries will change "tours" in our next edition. (We will change their classification because they yelled at us and we are weak, or they have changed their hours of operation and/or moved to new facilities, or have become extinct and thus become members of our elite cemetery wine association.)

Washington Wine Country Fact One
Washington is the second largest premium wine producer in the United States with over six hundred wineries and three hundred and fifty wine grape growers. (washingtonwine.org)

The Wine Tour

Walla Walla Wineries

Amavi Cellars (2001)
635 N. 13th Ave.
Walla Walla, WA 99362
509-525-3541
www.amavicellars.com
Hours: 11:00 am to 5:00 pm (Daily)

Amavi Cellars is a combination of old Latin root words "am" (love), and "vi" (life). On their label is the Roman goddess of agriculture (Ceres), which symbolizes their commitment to sustainable viticulture.

Three families (Goff, McKibben and Pellet) are partners in the Amavi Cellars project. The estate vineyards Les Collines, Seven Hills and Pepper Bridge are farmed sustainably and Jean Francoise Pellet is winemaker.

The tasting room is a reconstructed 1890s log cabin built with twice-recycled, hand-hewn lumber. The exterior resembles an early twentieth century Walla Walla storefront.

Amavi is a member of Vinea which is a "voluntary group of winegrowers that have embraced a covenant with environmental, economic and social sustainability concurrent with their production of grapes and wine." (www.vineatrust.org)

Seven Hills Vineyard by Alexei Kazantsev

Canoe Ridge Winery (1989)
1102 W. Cherry St.
Walla Walla, WA 99362
509-527-0885
www.canoeridgevineyard.com
Hours: 11:00 am to 5:00 pm (Daily)

In 1989, Phil Woodward, co-founder of Chalone wine group, and local Walla Walla investors, including Rick Small of Woodward Canyon, purchased Canoe Ridge Vineyard located on the northern bank of the Columbia River. The land was changed from a home for badgers, snakes and sagebrush to one hundred forty-three acres of vineyards.

The name comes from a ridge located on the eastern Washington side of the Columbia River. Lewis and Clark named this crest of land as they journeyed down the Columbia River in 1805. From the river the explorers thought the ridge looked like an overturned canoe. (Information comes from Canoe Ridge website.)

Canoe Ridge is one of the larger wineries in the Walla Walla Valley with a production of 30,000 cases per year with an emphasis on Merlot. The winery is a converted Walla Walla engine house.

Note: Some have asked if the two people in the canoe are Sam and Dave. We believe the inspiration for the label came from Lewis and Clark, primarily because the canoe looks vintage 1805 and our canoe is much newer. Extra note: Some people say Sam and Dave look newer than 1805 as well. We couldn't get a consensus on this however.

Washington Wine Country Fact Two

In 2008 Washington harvested a record 145,000 tons of grapes.

Top five red varietals – Cabernet Sauvignon, Merlot, Syrah, Cabernet Franc and Malbec.

Top five white varietals – Riesling, Chardonnay, Sauvignon Blanc, Pinot Gris and Gewurztraminer.   (washingtonwine.org)

L'Ecole No 41 (1983)
41 Lowden School Rd.
Lowden, WA 99360
509-525-0940
www.lecole.com
Hours: 10:00 am to 5:00 pm (Daily)

In 1984 a man walked into my retail wine shop and asked if I had any Gewurztraminer. He walked out with a case of wine that included Beaucastel Chateauneuf du Pape, Gaja Barbaresco, Trimbach Gewurztraminer and Merlots from Pomerol, France and California. Baker Ferguson said he and his wife, Jean, were making wine in a school house in Lowden, Washington. A year later I visited them. His wines weren't filtered. Baker smiled when he said the Merlot had a lot of "stuff" on the sides of the bottle. The Gewurztraminer was in oak. I liked the Merlot but more than that I liked the vision. He wanted to make the best wines possible and restore an historical site in the process.

L'Ecole was founded in 1983 by Baker and Jean Ferguson. In 1989 their son-in-law Marty Clubb took over as owner-winemaker. Along with his wife, Megan, they continued the quest that Megan's parents had started in 1983. They combined their energy to learn all aspects of the wine industry and their talents for business to rebuild the 1915 Lowden School. They set goals for their brand – goals that would not only propel their wine onto the national scene but also provide a model for many of the upcoming Walla Walla wineries to build on. Many of the wineries in the Walla Walla Valley have links to L'Ecole and Woodward Canyon, two of the pioneers in the Washington wine industry, the bios read "a former assistant winemaker at L'Ecole …"

Marty spent much of his time doing winemaker dinners and tastings throughout the United States as a strategy to develop his brand in the upper niche of the wine industry. Kim Clothier was hired to market the brand nationally and internationally.

As this marketing strategy evolved Marty also partnered with Gary Figgins of Leonetti and Norm McKibben of Pepper Bridge to purchase Seven Hills Vineyard. In 1980 when Baker Ferguson started formulating his winery idea there were twenty producing wineries in the state of Washington; now there are more than one hundred wineries in the Walla Walla Valley appellation alone! L'Ecole is also a member of Vinea. (For more information on Vinea see our glossary or go to www.vineatrust.com)

A visit to the tasting room is a small window into the history of Walla Walla Valley wines. They produce a wide variety of red and white wines including two reserve blends from Seven Hills Vineyard and Pepper Bridge Vineyard – Apogee and Perigee.

In 1984 an art contest was held among the elementary children in the extended family. The winner was 8 year old cousin Ryan Campbell. His watercolor became the focus of the label. Marty and Megan's children, Riley and Rebecca, have added touches of their own to the label. In memory of Megan's mother and founding winemaker, Jean Ferguson, a guardian angel appears in the lower right hand corner of label, beginning with the 1998 Seven Hills Vineyard Merlot. (For more information and colored picture visit L'Ecole's website.)

Morrison Lane (2002)
201 W. Main St.
Walla Walla, WA 99362
509-526-0229
www.morrisonlane.com
Hours: 12:00 pm to 5:00 pm (Friday-Monday)

The Morrison family farms date back to 1918. In 1997 Dean Morrison began changing some of the focus of the farm and planted grapes for Walla Walla wineries. His wife Verdie is an integral part of the winery's marketing and along with their son, Dan, shares the winemaking duties. Dan learned his craft from John Abbott at Canoe Ridge.

Morrison Lane lives up to the expectations of wine, food and music. Dean is a bass player and his son Dan is a guitar player. You will find northwest jazz musicians and local residents visiting the home town tasting room. Dean and Verdie's other two children, Dinah and Sean, also help with the production, marketing and special events. Visiting the Morrison Lane tasting room will also give you a chance to taste some of the newest varietals in the Walla Walla Valley appellation including Counoise, Cinsault, Syrah, Carmenere, Rousanne, Viognier, Dolcetto, Nebbiolo, Sangiovese and Barbera.

Dean & Verdie Morrison

Pepper Bridge Winery (1998)
1704 JB George Rd.
Walla Walla, WA 99362
509-525-6502
www.pepperbridge.com
Hours: 10:00 am to 4:00 pm (Daily)

Pepper Bridge Winery produces estate vineyard wines from Seven Hills Vineyard and Pepper Bridge Vineyard in the Walla Walla Valley appellation. That would be enough said for most but owner, Norm McKibben, should have his own chapter in a history of the Washington State wine industry

Norm has been a partner in Hogue Cellars in Prosser and Canoe Ridge Vineyard in Walla Walla. In 1994 he purchased Seven Hills Vineyard and his own Pepper Bridge Winery was completed in 2000.

Much of Norm's current involvement in the wine industry is based around his partnerships in vineyards like Pepper Bridge, Seven Hills and Les Collines. He focuses on growing grapes to the specifications of his wineries like Leonetti, L'Ecole #41, Andrew Will and Grande Ronde Cellars. His vineyards have state-of-the-art soil moisture, temperature, and irrigation monitoring equipment.

Pepper Bridge vineyard uses cutting-edge technology irrigation and weather systems. You can get round the clock updates of weather on their website.

Norm is a member of Vinea and a leader in sustainable growing practices. The vineyard applies compost tea through their drip irrigation system and plants wild roses to provide winter habitat for a parasitic wasp that attacks leaf hoppers. The website is worth visiting before you visit the winery not only because it gives you some information about Pepper Bridge but it will help you understand the evolving wine industry in the Walla Walla Valley. I mean, leaving weeds for beneficial insects, I wish I would have come up with that idea at home.

Seven Hills Winery (1988)
212 N. Third Ave.
Walla Walla, WA 99362
509-529-7198
www.sevenhillswinery.com
Hours: 11:00 am to 4:00 pm (Thurs-Sat and Monday)

Casey McClellan cultivated his interest in wines while planting the first block of Seven Hills Vineyard in the early 1980s. He went on to earn a master's degree from the University of California at Davis specializing in the study of wine yeast performance. In 1988, Casey returned to the Walla Walla Valley to join the vineyard's founding partners and establishing Seven Hills Winery.

I started working with Casey when his winery was located in Milton-Freewater, Oregon. It was the fifth winery in the Walla Walla AVA. My entire staff was stranded on top of an apple packing building (Seven Hills original winery location) while we waited for the freight elevator to get fixed. We went up there to see how beautiful the valley looked from one of the highest spots in Milton Freewater. It looked like a long jump to the ground for awhile. From that building in Milton-Freewater, Oregon to his tasting room and winery facility in Walla Walla Casey has left his own special mark on the Walla Walla Valley.

Casey produces a Pinot Gris and White Riesling to go with his Cabernet Sauvignon, Merlot and Syrah wines. He has always sought to make the wines accessible at an early age and thus gained a lot of support from restaurants for their quality/price ratio. Casey has also been experimenting with varietals like Malbec and Tempranillo. You will see the name Seven Hills in the bios of many other wineries. It all started here with Casey and his family – many of the accolades that wineries have achieved in Walla Walla can be traced back to the vision of the McClellan clan.

Photo by Colby Kuschatka

Woodward Canyon Winery (1981)
11920 W. Hwy. 12
Lowden, WA 99360
509-525-4129
www.woodwardcanyon.com
Hours: 10:00 am to 5:00 pm (Daily)

Rick Small, and his wife, Darcy Fugman-Small started Woodward Canyon in 1981. Woodward Canyon was a founding member of the Walla Walla Valley Wine Alliance and has been instrumental in developing the Walla Walla Valley appellation name. They were one of the first wineries in Washington to be rated in the top ten of the *Wine Spectator's* top one hundred wines. Along with Leonetti Cellars, Woodward Canyon helped put Walla Walla on the world wine radar screen.

The tasting room is in a restored 1870s farmhouse next to the highway in Lowden. Woodward Canyon is also noted for its support of artists through its "Artist Series" Cabernet Sauvignon releases.

Woodward Canyon has always been about the vineyards. Rick sources several vineyards including his own estate vineyard in Lowden, Washington which is about 900 feet in elevation. The vineyard was planted in 1977 on third generation family land. The vineyard is in the process of becoming an International Organization for Biological Control (IOBC) vineyard. The IOBC was established in 1955 to promote environmentally safe methods to control pests and diseases.

Rick also partnered with Quilceda Creek, Andrew Will, Badger Mountain and Paul Champoux to purchase Champoux Vineyard, one of the oldest vineyards in the state. Champoux was originally Mercer Ranch Vineyard which was planted in 1972. The Mercer family farms have been a part of Eastern Washington agriculture since the late 19th century.

Washington Wine Country Fact Three

Fort Nez Perce (later changed to Fort Walla Walla) was a fur trading post established in 1818. Walla Walla was incorporated in 1862 and currently is home to Whitman College, Walla Walla University, one hundred wineries and the state penitentiary.

Part II – The Geek Tour

428 Winery (2004)
675 E St. (airport)
PO Box 308
Walla Walla, WA 99362
509-552-8486
www.428wines.com

Winemaker Jeff Sully and his wife, Kim, released their inaugural vintage of 428, a 2004 blend of Merlot with Syrah called Boulevard, in 2008. It was aged for 22 months in new and old French oak. They also produce "L'avenue," a classic Bordeaux white wine blend of Sauvignon Blanc and Semillon.

Abeja (2002)
2014 Mill Creek Rd.
Walla Walla, WA 99362
509-526-7400
www.abeja.net

The name of Abeja (ah-bay-ha) comes from the Spanish word for bee. The word was chosen to honor the contributions of Latino workers in the wine industry. The bee represents the owners' respect for the land and their desire to work in tandem with nature. John Abbott, Molly Galt, Ken and Ginger Harrison are partners at Abeja.

Jacob Kibler filed for a homestead in the Walla Walla Valley in 1863 claiming 160 acres on Mill Creek. Those 160 acres eventually turned into thousands of acres of wheat and timberland and farm buildings built between 1903 and 1907. In 2000 Ken and Ginger Harrison purchased the farm which included forty-two acres of the original Kibler farmstead.

The winery is in a building that was originally used as the mule and horse barn of the Kibler Farm. The Inn at Abeja is a turn of the century farmstead surrounded by 35 acres of gardens, creeks and vineyards for guests to explore.

àMaurice Cellars (2004)
178 Vineyard Ln.
Walla Walla, WA 99362
509-522-5444
www.amaurice.com

àMaurice Cellars is owned by the Schafer family. The winery and Vineyards are located in the foothills of the Blue Mountains. Tom, Kathleen, Anna, Nicholas and Stephanie are the founding partners; Anna Schafer is the winemaker. Anna works the harvest in Mendoza, Argentina for winemaker Paul Hobb's Vina Cobos. àMaurice is producing a Chardonnay, Viognier, Merlot, Malbec, Syrah and a red blend, "the Callahan."

Adamant Cellars (2006)
600 Piper Ave. (airport)
Walla Walla, WA 99362
509-529-4161
www.adamantcellars.com

Devon and Debra Stinger began their winemaking career in the basement of their home in Portland, Oregon. Adamant is a doublet for diamond. The name implies a hearty substance with power and depth, which is what they are striving for in their wines. Adamant cellars produce a Syrah, Cabernet Sauvignon blend and a Sauvignon Blanc/Semillon blend.

Artifex Winery (2007)
1102 Dell Ave.
Walla Walla, WA 99362
509-525-2469

Artifex is a custom crush winery created by Jean-Francois Pellet, winemaker at Pepper Bridge Winery, Norm McKibben, partner in Pepper Bridge Cellars and Amavi, together with Rick Middleton who runs an agribusiness firm. The manager and winemaker is Chris Dowsett formerly with Canoe Ridge and Latitude 46. The goal of the winery is to provide service to people who are new to the industry and want to produce a wine, but aren't ready to build their own facilities.

Ash Hollow (2002)
14 N. Second Ave.
Walla Walla, WA 99362
509-529-7565
www.ashhollow.com

John Turner is Ash Hollow's managing partner, and Steve Clifton is the consulting winemaker/partner. Their philosophy is that wines are made in the vineyard and should reflect the character of the site. Winemaking is minimalist and traditional with a New World attitude. John and his wife, Jacqui, are fourth generation Walla Walla-ites. Their winemaker/partner is Justin Michaud.

Balboa Winery (2004)
7 S. Fourth
Walla Walla, WA 99362
509-529-0461
www.balboawinery.com

Balboa was started by Mike Sharon and Tom Glase with the intent purpose of bringing wine to the "masses." Tom uses screw cap closures on his Balboa wines, making it easy for everyone to enjoy the distinct wines of Washington. Amy Glase, Tom's wife, is the artist who designs the Balboa labels.

Basel Cellars (2002)
2901 Old Milton Hwy.
Walla Walla, WA 99362
888-259-9463
www.baselcellars.com

Basel Cellars is a 13,500 square-foot wine country resort. The estate features luxury overnight accommodations for up to 18 guests in the rustic yet elegant facility. Although this was once a member's only private estate, visitors are now welcome in the tasting room which is open seven days a week. Greg Basel is the owner.

Beresan Winery (2001)
4169 Pepper Bridge Rd.
Walla Walla, WA 99362
509-522-2395
www.beresanwines.com

Tom Waliser named the winery after the region in the Ukraine close to the Black Sea where his family emigrated from Germany in the early 1800s. The family landed in Walla Walla in 1931. Beresan's grapes are from their 18 acres of estate vineyard. Waliser Vineyard is the original flagship vineyard for the winery. Yellow Jacket Vineyard was a peach and apple orchard before being planted into grapes. The Beresan estate vineyard is comprised of Cabernet Franc and Semillon. Some fruit has also been used from Pepper Bridge and Candy Mountain Vineyards, which are managed by Beresan's owner Tom Waliser.

Bergevin Lane Vineyards (2002)
1215 W. Poplar St.
Walla Walla, WA 99362
509-526-4300
www.bergevinlane.com

Gary Bergevin has been a director of Sandpipers Farms, the site of Canoe Ridge Vineyard since 1972. He was a founding partner of Canoe Ridge Vineyard in 1988 and in 2001 Gary became a partner and CFO of Forgeron Cellars. He formed Bergevin Lane Vineyards with Amber Lane and his daughter Annette Bergevin. The winemaker is Steffan Jorgenson.

Berghan Vineyards
4625 Braden Rd.
Walla Walla, WA 99362

Berghan Vineyards is a bonded Washington Winery. It was the beginnings of Gifford Hirlinger where Mike Berghan is winemaker.

Bodega Turner (2001)
222 Main St.
Waitsburg, WA 99361
509-210-9900

Bodega Turner specialized in Bordeaux varietals with a special emphasis on Malbec. Holly Turner was a winemaker at Three Rivers Winery when she teamed with Michael to start Bodega Turner. They both have worked in wineries in Argentina, France and Washington State. Michael Turner moved the business to Waitsburg, WA.

Bradenview Cellars
305 E. Boeing Ave. (airport)
Walla Walla, WA 99362
509-529-7264

Bradenview Cellars makes Bordeaux style red wines including a 2003 blend called Casilda.

Bunchgrass Winery

See the Cemetery. After two years of being buried this winery is being revived by former owner Roger Cockerline with new partners, Bill von Metzger as winemaker, Tom Olander and Barb Commare. This is a Geek's dream. More in the next edition in our double Geek Tour.

Buty Winery (2000)
535 E. Cessna Ave. (airport)
Walla Walla, WA 99362
509-527-0901
www.butywinery.com

Caleb Foster has worked for twenty years in wineries throughout the world including New Zealand, South Africa and the United States. Nina Buty Foster is co-owner and contributes her artistic visions to Buty wines. She plans to pursue an outdoor sculpture garden at the winery. They have two vineyards, Phinny Hill and Rockgarden.

Cadaretta (2008)
1102 Dell Ave.
Walla Walla, WA 99362
509-591-0324
www.cadaretta.com

Cadaretta is a new Walla Walla winery, combining a family agricultural history with an "international" wine style. Owned by Rick Middleton and family, the name comes from an Anderson-Middleton schooner that traveled the west coast in the early 20th century. Virginie Bourgue is Cadaretta's winemaker. Cadaretta makes a Sauvignon Blanc-Semillon blend, a Syrah, a Chardonnay and Merlot.

Cavu Cellars (2008)
602 Piper Ave.
Walla Walla, WA 99326

Joel Waite has partnered with his parents, Jim and Karen Waite, to open Cavu Cellars. The winery name is an aeronautical acronym for Ceiling and Visibility Unlimited (paying homage to Jim Waite's career as a pilot).

Cayuse Vineyards (1997)
17 E. Main St.
Walla Walla, WA 99362
509-526-0686
www.cayusevineyards.com

Christophe Baron studied viticulture in his native France. He came to the United States in 1993 to train at Adelsheim in Oregon and Waterbrook Winery in Lowden, WA. He specializes in vineyard-designated Syrah. His vineyard is located fifteen miles south of Walla Walla. He replanted an orchard which was covered with cobblestones similar to the terroir of Chateauneuf-du-Pape.

The riverbed was home to a Native American tribe the French-Canadian fur traders called Caillous (plural for "stone" in French). The tribe became known as the Cayuse. Cayuse Vineyards expanded its operations to include ten additional acres of vineyard called En Cerise and another ten acres called Coccinelle in 1997. The majority of the vineyards are planted in Syrah and some experimental plantings of Rousanne, Tempranillo and Viognier. In 2001 they planted Grenache, Syrah and Mourvedre in a new vineyard called Armada. They were the first to farm in Walla Walla using biodynamic methods.

Chateau Rollat Winery (2004)
1050 Merlot Dr.
Walla Walla, WA 99362
509-529-4511
www.rollat.com

Owner Bowin Lindgren hired consulting winemaker, Christian LeSommer (who had Chateau d'Yquem and Chateau Latour on his resume) in 2004 for the Chateau Rollat project. Their first release was a 2005 Cabernet Sauvignon from Pepper Bridge and Seven Hills Vineyards.

The winery is named after Lindgren's great grandparent, Edouard Rollat, who came to America in 1903. He came from a family of wine producers in France and western Switzerland. He became the wine sommelier at Café Martin on 27th Street in Manhattan. He became a wine educator during prohibition and after its repeal he became a consultant for wineries, wrote articles and taught about wine.

College Cellars of Walla Walla (2003)
500 Tausick Way
Walla Walla, WA 99362
509-524-5170
www.collegecellars.com

College Cellars is both a teaching and commercial winery. The wines are crafted by students while completing their studies in the science of winemaking. Their 2008 releases included a 2006 Governor's Red and a 2007 Governor's White. The advisory committee is made up of people in the local wine industry, including winemakers and owners.

Corliss Estates
511 N. Second Ave.
Walla Walla WA 99362
509-526-4400

Michael Corliss is the owner and Kendall Mix is the winemaker. The winery is located in an old bakery building which has been turned into a state of the art winery. Corliss is releasing their 2004 Syrah in 2009. Currently almost their entire production is sold via their mailing list.

Cougar Crest Winery (2001)
50 Frenchtown Rd. (off Highway 12)
Walla Walla, WA 99362
509-529-5980
www.cougarcrestwinery.com

Cougar Crest owners, Deborah and David Hansen, are Northwest natives and graduates of Washington State University. Deborah Hansen is the winemaker and started her training at the University of California Davis. Cougar Crest Winery is focusing on 100% estate wines in the Walla Walla Valley. All of the estate fruit is organically grown. They produce Cabernet Sauvignon, Syrah, Cabernet Franc, Merlot and Viognier.

Couvillion (2005)
86 Corkrum Rd.
Walla Walla, WA 99362
509-377-6133
www.couvillionwinery.com

Couvillion (pronounced "Coo-vee-on") is named for Winemaker Jill Nobel's friend, Connie O'Neill of Louisiana. "It is her family name. "It is French-Canadian, and I wanted to honor her because she is so dear to my heart," says Jill. The winery produces Cabernet Sauvignon, Merlot and Sauvignon Blanc.

DaMa Wines (2007)
45 E. Main St.
Walla Walla, WA 99362
509-520-9687
www.damawines.com

    DaMa wines are based on the French negociant model in which the owners blend small lots of select wines. Dawn Kammer and Mary Derby started their enterprise with a goal to reach out to women who are interested in wine no matter what their level of wine experience. DaMa joins the first two letters of the women's names, and is Spanish for lady "defined as refined and well-spoken." (DaMa site)

Doubleback Winery (2007)
Future Site of Winery – McQueen Vineyard
509-301-3477
www.doubleback.com

    Doubleback Winery is Drew and Maura Bledsoe's winery. The wine will be made with fruit from various vineyards in the Walla Walla appellation and from their estate vineyard, McQueen, which was planted in 2008. They plan to release their first wine in 2010. Drew is a Walla Walla native who played football at Washington State University and was the number one draft pick in the 1993 NFL draft. Chris Figgins is their consulting winemaker. They are currently not open to the public.

Dowsett Family Winery (2007)
1102 Dell Ave.
Walla Walla, WA 99326
509-520-8215
www.dowsettwines.com

    Chris Dowsett produces a Celilo Vineyard Gewurztraminer and a Rhone blend. Chris worked at Canoe Ridge Vineyards before being named the winemaker at the Artifex.

Dumas Station Wines (2006)
36229 Highway 12
Dayton, WA 99328
509-382-8933
www.dumasstation.com

The winery and tasting room are located in the historic Dumas Station (a packing warehouse established by James Dumas in 1897) twenty-six miles northeast of downtown Walla Walla. They produce an estate grown Cabernet Sauvignon.

Dunham Cellars (1999)
150 E. Boeing (airport)
Walla Walla, WA 99362
509-529-4685
www.dunhamcellars.com

Eric Dunham was an assistant winemaker at L'Ecole #41 for four years before opening his own winery. He produces Cabernet Sauvignon, Syrah, Semillon and a Bordeaux blend. The address is also the home of Trey Marie Winery. In 2008 Dan Wampfler became the winemaker at Dunham Cellars after receiving his undergraduate and master's degrees from the University of Michigan.

Dusted Valley Vintners (2002)
1248 Old Milton Hwy.
Walla Walla, WA 99362
509-525-1337
www.dustedvalley.com

The winery (owned by the Chad Johnson and Corey Braunel clans from Wisconsin) is known for concentrated Syrah (you can join their Stained Tooth Society). They purchased Bradenview Vineyard and renamed it Sconni Block Vineyard. They are unique in that their oak comes from Wisconsin (cheese head aging?). Part of the oak is from their families' land in Wisconsin.

El Corazon (2006)
37 S. Palouse St.
Walla Walla, WA 99362
785-760-0326
www.elcorazonwinery.com

Raul Mortin and winemaker Spencer Sievers have teamed up to start El Corazon. The winery produces Sangiovese red and rose. Both Flying Trout Wines and Reininger have helped El Corazon in their wine project.

El Mirador (2000)
425 B Street (airport)
Walla Walla, WA 99362
509-526-0233

Owners Joe and Amy Donnow have opened a tasting room at the old Preston location in Walla Walla. The name comes from Amy's grandfather who grew up in a house in Ojai Valley, California named El Mirador. They produce Merlot, Cabernet Sauvignon and a red blend, "Campesino" (Counnoise, Cinsault and Syrah).

Elegante Cellars (2006)
839 C Street (airport)
Walla Walla, WA 99362
509-629-3735
www.elegantecellars.com

Owner/winemaker Doug Simmons is a retired teacher. Doug received a certificate of Viticulture from Walla Walla Community College and worked at Five Star Cellars before opening his own venture. He has produced an off-dry Gewurztraminer, Merlot (Seven Hills Vineyard) and 2007 Cabernet Sauvignon (Les Collines Vineyard).

Washington Wine Country Fact Four

The 2006 vintage saw 120,000 tons of grapes harvested, up 9% from the previous vintage.

Ensemble Cellars (2004)
145 East Curtis Ave. (airport)
Walla Walla, WA 99362
509-525-0231
www.ensemblecellars.com

Craig Nelson and his wife, Bunny, are the owners of Ensemble Cellars. Craig started out at Walla Walla Vintners and then worked as an assistant winemaker at Nicholas Cole. The winery blends wine from different vintages to produce their Ensemble wine. They currently have released three wines – Release One, Release Two and not to confuse you, Release Three. They range from Release Number One's makeup of 68% (2003 vintage) and 32% (2004 vintage) – a blend of 60% Cabernet Sauvignon, 24% Merlot and 16% Cabernet Franc to Release Number Three which is 13% (2004), 56% (2005) and 31% (2006) with the fruit coming from twelve different blocks of fruit including Sagemoor, Canoe Ridge, Dubrul and Red Mountain Vineyards.

Five Star Cellars (2001)
840 C Street (airport)
Walla Walla, WA 99362
509-527-8400
www.fivestarcellars.com

The Huse families are natives of Walla Walla and have been making wine since 2000. Begun by David Huse the winemaking is now handled by son Matt. Matt graduated from Walla Walla High School in 1996. He entered the viticulture program at Walla Walla Community College in 2001. The entire family is involved in the operation. Five Star Cellars produces red wines – Cabernet Sauvignon, Merlot, Malbec and Syrah produced from Walla Walla Valley fruit.

Washington Wine Country Fact Five

The 2004 vintage saw a decrease in the total number of tons harvested. An arctic freeze in October of 2003 caused many of the vineyards to suffer damage in the Walla Walla Valley area.

Flying Trout Wines (2004)
37 South Palouse St.
Walla Walla, WA 99362
509-520-7701
www.flyingtroutwines.com

Flying Trout Wines is a tiny bi-hemispherical winery based in both Walla Walla, Washington and Mendoza, Argentina. With Malbecs from the two regions as well as Syrahs from both sides of the equator FTW hopes to craft equally delicious futures out of drastically different pasts. Winemaker Ashley Trout travels to Argentina every year from February through May to work in the Mendoza Valley.

Forgeron Cellars (2001)
33 W. Birch St.
Walla Walla, WA 99362
509-522-9463
www.forgeroncellars.com

Forgeron is French for blacksmith. They contract with different vineyards throughout the Columbia and Walla Walla Valley to produce wines that reflect the terroirs of the area. A renovated, turn-of-the-century blacksmith shop houses their tasting room and winery. Maria Eva Gault, owner/winemaker produces Cabernet Sauvignon, Merlot, Syrah and Chardonnay.

Fort Walla Walla Cellars (1998)
1383 Barleen Dr.
Walla Walla, WA 99362
509-520-1095
www.fortwallawallacellars.com

Fort Walla Walla Cellars has a downtown Walla Walla tasting room at 127 E. Main. Fort Walla Walla was built to support the fur trade in 1818. (This was almost 20 years before the Whitman Mission in 1836.) It was first called Fort Nez Perce by the Hudson Bay Company and manned by French Canadian trappers. It is believed to be the site of the first vineyards in the area. Jim Moyer and Cliff Kontos are the winemakers.

Foundry Vineyards (2003)
13th and Abadie St.
Walla Walla, WA 99362
509-529-0736
www.foundryvineyards.com

The winery is located within Foundry Gallery, exhibiting artists working with the Walla Walla foundry. Owner and winemaker Mark Anderson produces a Cabernet Sauvignon-Merlot blend from Walla Walla Valley grapes.

Gardena Creek Winery (2005)
1211 Gardena Creek Rd.
Touchet, WA 99360
509-632-1328
www.gardenacreekwinery.com

Michael and Sharon Ingham are the owners of Gardena Creek Winery. All fruit is sourced from Gardena Creek Vineyards.

Garrison Creek Cellars (2001)
4137 Hood Rd.
Walla Walla, WA 99362
509-386-4841

Garrison Creek has a Cabernet Sauvignon, Syrah, Zinfandel and red blends. Michael Murr is the owner. The winery opening is a case study in zoning laws. The original 15,000 square-foot main floor and 10,000 square-foot cellar have been pared back to allow the winery in the previously exclusive agriculture area, which included rock quarries and private airstrips. Les Collines Vineyard in the foothills of the Blue Mountains has long been an interesting project.

An Idaho Fact -- In 2008 the Snake River Valley AVA was established making it the first AVA in Idaho. The Snake River Valley AVA covers more than five million acres making it half the size of Washington's Columbia Valley AVA.

Gifford Hirlinger (2001)
1450 Stateline Rd.
Walla Walla, WA 99362
509-529-2075
www.giffordhirlinger.com

This winery has released a Merlot, a Cabernet Sauvignon and a blend called "Stateline Red." Eventually all of their wines will be produced from fruit off their own 15 acre estate vineyard in Walla Walla. In 2001, the Berghan family planted their estate vineyard and chose their ancestral families (who came to Walla Walla in the mid-1800s) of Gifford and Hirlinger to use as their winery name. Mike Berghan is the winemaker.

Glen Fiona (1994)
1249 Lyday Lane
Walla Walla, WA 99362
509-522-2566
www.glenfiona.com

The Glen Fiona label has an interesting story. The intertwined border of Celtic knots which have no end is a symbol of longevity. The font for 'Glen Fiona' is adapted from old Irish script and represents the name's Gaelic origins meaning "Valley of the Vine." The ellipsoidal woodcut is a 17th century work that depicts an old world grapevine, trained up a single stake, which overlooks a valley vineyard and winery. The solitary grapevine is an antiquarian symbol of patience. Glen Fiona was one of the first wineries to produce Syrah in Walla Walla.

The original name of the winery was Blue Mountain Cellars and had five owners. In January of 1998 the partnership was reduced to two partners, David Weeks and Ronald White. Rusty Figgins was the original winemaker and was replaced by Caleb Foster. The label was purchased by Silver Lake in 2004. The current winemaker is William Ammons.

Gramercy Cellars (2005)
1825 JB George Rd.
Walla Walla, WA 99362
www.gramercycellars.com

Owner and winemaker Greg Harrington, MS, (in 1996 the youngest American to pass the Masters Sommelier exam) has had a colorful career managing wine programs for celebrity chefs. He founded the winery in 2005 with wife Pam. The goal is to "produce the best, most balanced, terroir-driven wines with minimal intervention."

Grande Ronde Cellars (1997)
201 W. Main St.
Walla Walla, WA 99326
509-526-0229
www.granderondecellars.com

Grande Ronde Cellars has opened a tasting room with Morrison Lane at the downtown Walla Walla location. Grande Ronde produces wines from two of the most famous vineyards in the Walla Walla Valley appellation, Seven Hills Vineyard and Pepper Bridge Vineyard. Their wines have received numerous 90 plus scores in the *Wine Spectator*. See Grande Ronde under Spokane wineries for more information.

Grantwood Cellars
W. 2428 Hwy. 12
Walla Walla, WA

Applied for use permit in 2007

Harlequin Wine Cellars (1999)
1211 Sand Pit Rd.
Touchet, WA 99360
877-432-3237
www.harlequinwine.com

Harlequin Wine Cellars is owned by winemaker Robert Goodfriend and his wife, Elizabeth. Robert previously apprenticed at

Wild Horse in California, and Silvan Ridge in Oregon. Harlequin makes Cabernet Sauvignon, Merlot and Syrah from Washington State, and Pinot Noir from Oregon.

Harrison Cellars (2007)
1050 Merlot Dr.
Walla Walla, WA 99326
Applied for Use Permit in 2007

Hence Cellars (2005)
4122 Powerline Rd.
Walla Walla, WA 99362
509-529-4010

The winery is in an 8000 sq/ft. log building with a copper colored roof. Henderson Orchard is the owner and Troy Ledwich is the winemaker. Hence Cellars is producing a Syrah, Cabernet Sauvignon and Malbec from their estate Vineyard, as well as wines from Columbia Valley fruit.

Isenhower Winery (1999)
3471 Pranger Rd.
Walla Walla, WA 99362
509-526-7896
www.isenhowercellars.com

Denise and Brett Isenhower crushed their first grapes in the fall of 1999 at Glen Fiona. They have backgrounds that included both chemistry and business. By 2002 they had moved into their current facility on six acres of farmland south of Walla Walla. They planted two acres of Malbec in 2008, with plans to increase their vineyard size. They produce Cabernet Sauvignon, Merlot and Syrah. They are also experimenting with Grenache, Rousanne and Viognier.

Washington Wine Country Fact Six

The 2005 vintage returned to normal with 116,000 tons harvested. Up 15% from the 2004 vintage which had experienced the first significant decrease in production since the 1996 vintage.

JLC Winery (2001)
426 B Street (airport)
Walla Walla, WA 99326
509-529-1398
www.jlcwinery.com

James Leigh Cellars was started in 2001 by Lynne Chamberlain, James Brown and Leigh Brown. Lynne Chamberlain is now the owner of the winery. JLC has forty acres of estate vineyards, the Spofford Station Estate Vineyard. The tasting room gallery features several original works of art by local painter and winemaker Leigh Brown. James Leigh Cellars produces a Cabernet Sauvignon, Syrah and Bordeaux blend.

James Leigh Cellars (2001)

See: JLC Winery

James Waite Cellars
360 B St.
Walla Walla, WA 99362

K Vintners (2001)
820 Mill Creek Rd. (airport)
Walla Walla, WA 99326
509-526-5230
www.kvintners.com

Eclectic owner/winemaker Charles Smith produces a variety of wines, but is most well known for limited-production Syrah with names like "The Boy," "The Creator," and "The Beautiful." He also makes wines under the Charles Smith label including "Kung fu Girl Riesling," "Velvet Devil Merlot," and "Boom Boom Syrah." The Magnificent Wine Company portfolio was sold to Precept Wine Brands in 2008.

Kontos Cellars (2008)
594 Piper Ave.
Walla Walla, WA 99326
509-386-4471
www.kontoscellars.com

Cameron and Chris Kontos are producing wines under two different labels — Kontos Cellars and LeeVeLooLee. They are producing single varietal wines under the Kontos label and blended wines under the LeeVeLooLee label. Cameron has been an assistant for Marie-Eve Gilla at Forgeron as well as working with his brother at their father's winery, Fort Walla Walla Cellars.

K-W Cellars
1753 Old Milton Hwy.
Walla Walla, WA 99362
509-525-6222

Bonded winery in Washington State.

Lahar Winery (2004)
PO Box 2846
Walla Walla, WA 99362
509-240-4854

Tom Bronkema is the owner of Lahar. It is named after the Skagit Valley volcanic soil (lahars is volcanic mudflow). If one was going to be subtle about Bronkema's plans it would be that he is a Pinot Noir fanatic,

Laht Neppur Cellars (2009)
444 Preston Ave.
Waitsburg, WA 99361
509-337-6261
www.lahtneppur.com

Brewmaster/winemaker Court Ruppenthal released his first wine, a Port-style Syrah named Ocourto 4. He is planning to release a Cabernet Sauvignon in May, 2009.

Latitude 46 North (2002)
1211 Sand Pit Rd.
Touchet, WA 99360
253-874-1422
www.latitude46.com

Latitude 46 is owned by four families. The name comes from the latitude 46 degree line that falls just south of Walla Walla. The winemaker and co-owner is Chris Dowsett. He worked for six years as an assistant winemaker at Canoe Ridge Vineyard.

Le Chateau Walla Walla (2008)
175 E Aeronca Ave (airport)
Walla Walla, WA 99362
509-956-9311
www.lechateauwinery.com

Owners of Le Chateau (Dick & Diane Hoch, Bob & Crista Whitelach) painted their building in the likeness of a neoclassical French chateau. Bruce Corneaux of Claar Cellars is the winemaker. Le Chateau is specializing in Bordeaux-style white and red blends, Sangiovese, Cabernet Franc, Malbec and Syrah.

Leonetti Cellars (1977)
1875 Foothills La.
Walla Walla, WA 99362
509-525-1428
www.leonetticellar.com

Founded in 1977 by Gary Figgins and his wife, Nancy, Leonetti Cellars is one of the pioneers in the Washington wine industry. Their son, Chris, and daughter, Amy have become integral parts of the winery.

Gary has been a proponent of low yield, high intensity fruit. He is known for using a variety of American and French oak. Figgins is a partner with Marty Clubb and Norm McKibben in Seven Hills Vineyard and has developed his own estate vineyards of Mill Creek Upland (located in the foothills of the Blue Mountains) and Loess Vineyard (planted on a hillside next to his winery) to help ensure he has consistent fruit sources. I believe that much of the Walla Walla Valley wine prestige has to be attributed to the success of Leonetti Cellars.

When I first met Gary he was still working the graveyard shift at the cannery. After the midnight shift Gary would make his wines in the "tack" building. From that small tack shed Gary has built a winery that includes underground caves, barrel cellar, crushing and production facilities and a tasting room. The winery is named after his maternal grandparents, Frank and Rose Leonetti.

Lodmell Cellars (2005)
598 Piper Ave. (airport)
Walla Walla, WA 99362
509-525-1285
www.lodmellcellars.com

Andrew Lodmell, winemaker, Kristie Lodmell Kirlin and Randy Kirlin are the owners of Lodmell Cellars. Lodmell's great grandfather settled thirty miles northwest of Walla Wall near Eureka, WA in the late 1800s. Currently about 30 acres have been planted at the estate vineyard site near Eureka on the lower Snake River.

Long Shadows (2003)
1604 Frenchtown Rd.
Walla Walla, WA 99362
509-526-0905
www.longshadows.com

Long Shadows Vintners is the brainstorm of Alan Shoup, former CEO of Stimson Lane. Celebrated international vintners each produce a single Columbia Valley wine under a separate and distinct label – Poets Leap Riesling, Armin Diel; Chester Kidder Cabernet blend, Gilles Nicault; Sequel Syrah, John Duval; Feather Cabernet Sauvignon, Randy Dunn; Pedestal Merlot blend, Michel Rolland; Pirouette Cabernet blend, Huneeus/Melka; and Saggi Sangiovese blend, Folonari.

Lullaby (2006)
1102 Dell Ave.
Walla Walla, WA 99362
509-386-1324

Owner/winemaker Virginie Bourgue is from the south of France. She started her own winery, Lullaby, in 2006. Virginie has also been an enologist for Château Ste Michelle and a winemaker at Bergevin Lane. Her first releases will be a Viognier and Rose in 2009 with a Merlot-Cabernet blend to follow in 2010.

Mad Car Wine Company (2005)
1050 Merlot Dr.
Walla Walla, WA 99326
509-526-6903

Steve Brooks is the owner and the wine after his daughters, Madeleine and Carolyn.

Mannina Cellars (2004)
760 C St. (airport)
Walla Walla, WA 99362
509-529-5760
www.manninacellars.com

The winery was named after the maternal grandmother of the winemaker Don Redman. Don worked as an environmental engineer with Boise Cascade. The winery makes Merlot, Sangiovese and a Red Blend called "Cali" from Walla Walla Vineyards including Pepper Bridge, Seven Hills, and Les Collines.

MPM Vintners (2006)

Turn Key Operation for winemaking services.

Located in the Crown Cork & Seal Building the principal owners are Jean-Francois Pellet, Norm McKibben and Rick Middleton. We include this listing to show you some of the aspects of a growing wine industry where people have a plan, get licensed and either continue with that plan or choose a different path.

This incubation center will spawn many wineries, some will be very small and you may never hear of them. (We try to include them here but they are a tricky barrel to catch). Some grow into full blown wineries. Our goal is to give you a clue about as many of these wineries as we can. As the information becomes available we will update our book. For more information on this partnership see Artifex under Walla Walla Wineries.

Nicholas Cole Cellars (2001)
229 E. Main St.
Walla Walla, WA 99362
509-525-0608
www.nicholascolecellars.com

Mike Neuffer started Nicholas Cole Cellars in 2001. He was a developer in Nevada before purchasing the site for the winery. The winery is named after Mike's children, Nicholas and Michelle Cole. The winery is surrounded by 40 acres of estate vineyards. Chris Camarda of Andrew Will Winery consults with owner-winemaker Neuffer to source fruit from different wine regions in Washington.

Northstar (1994)
1736 JB George Rd.
Walla Walla, WA 98930
866-486-7828
www.northstarmerlot.com

Northstar's first vintage was 1994. The new winery was built in 2002. Northstar's winemaker is David Merfield who has worked with consultant Jed Steele since 2001. (Jed Steele has been a winemaker and consultant to many wineries in California and Washington). The focus of the winery is Merlot, although they also produce a blend (Stella Maris).

NxNW (2005)
1102 Dell Ave.
Walla Walla, WA 99362
877-696-9123
www.nxnwwine.com

NxNW is another facet of the wine industry. A large winery, King Estate of Oregon, sees the Walla Walla Valley as an opportunity to increase their production and sales while utilizing their current national infrastructure and expertise for sales and marketing. NxNW is a member of the Walla Walla Wine Alliance and represents wines made from the "inland" grape growing appellation of the Columbia Valley. North by Northwest produces Cabernet Sauvignon and Syrah from both the Walla Walla Valley and Columbia Valley appellations. Lindsay Boudreaux is the winemaker. She worked at Jordan Winery in California before coming to NxNW.

Otis Kenyon (2004)
23 E. Main St.
Walla Walla, WA 99362
509-525-3505
www.otiskenyonwine.com

James Otis Kenyon was a dentist in the Walla Walla Valley in the early 1900s. James, it appears, burned his competitor's office to the ground and spent a period of time providing cheap dental care to the staff and patients of the nearby hospital. (Note to wineries: this accepted method of eliminating competition appears to have ended with the dentist.) Stephen Otis Kenyon, grandson, and Deborah Dunbar are owners.

Patit Creek Cellars (1999)
325 A St. (airport)
Walla Walla, WA 99362
509-522-4684
www.patitcreekcellars.com

The word Patit comes from French fur traders, who called the stream of water running through the area Petite Creek. It was later changed to Patit Creek by the pioneer farmers. The French cottage house winery sits on the Nez Perce Trail near where Lewis and Clark camped on expedition. The six original founding partners sold the winery to Karen La Bonte and Ed Dudley. In 2008 Karen and Ed moved the winery from Dayton to Walla Walla.

Patrick M. Paul Vineyards (1998)
107 S. Third Ave.
Walla Walla, WA 99362
509-526-0676
www.pmpvineyards.com

Mike Paul founded Patrick M. Paul Vineyards in 1986 and along with his wife, Teresa, started the winery in 1988. Patrick Paul's first production was Boysenberry and Concord dessert wines. He planted Cabernet Franc in 1984. The winery has been researching grape varietals since the early 1980s leading to vineyard plantings of Cabernet Franc, Pinot Noir, Merlot, Cabernet Sauvignon and Chardonnay. Mike Paul passed away in January, 2009. He was one of the earliest members of the Walla Walla wine community. He was a founding member of the Walla Walla Wine Alliance, was involved in the launch of Walla Walla Village Winery and was co-host of a Walla Walla radio show on wine.

River Raft Vintners (2008)
1102 Dell Ave.
Walla Walla, WA 99362

This winery has been bonded in Washington State and is owned by the Middleton family. You can see a video on You tube about the vineyards. www.youtube.com/user/vintagenewworld. Just another way the wine community can make its public more informed about the world of wine making.

Washington Wine Country Fact Seven

1996 was the greatest percentage in crop reduction from the previous vintage on record. Only 34,000 tons were harvested in 1996 compared to 62,000 tons in 1995.

Reininger Winery (1997)
5858 W. Hwy. 12
Walla Walla, WA 99362
509-522-1994
www.reiningerwinery.com

Owner-winemaker Chuck Reininger crafts mostly red wines from Pepper Bridge, Seven Hills and Spring Valley vineyards in Walla Walla. Chuck and wife Tracy partnered with Jay and Cyndi Tucker, Kelly and Ann Tucker (Tracy's two brothers and sisters-in-law) to work at the winery and purchased property in 2002 to plant Ash Hollow vineyard (280 acres at the West end of Walla Walla Valley), of which 39 acres have been planted with Cabernet Sauvignon, Merlot and Syrah vines.

Reynvaan Family Vineyards (2007)
6557 Cottonwood Rd.
Walla Walla, WA 99362
206-280-2715
www.reynvaanfamilyvineyards.com

Mike and Gale Reynvaan along with their three children, Amanda Carvalho, Angela Garratt and Matt, started Reynvaan Family Vineyards. Matt Reynvaan is the winemaker and vineyard manager. Reynvaan Family Vineyards produced two Syrahs in 2007, "Apollonius" (named after Apollonius Reynvaan who started a shipping and wine merchant company in the early 1800s in Hong Kong, China) and "In the Rocks" Vineyard. The winery will be built next to their "Foothills in the Sun" Vineyard at the base of the Blue Mountains. The initial release for their wines is projected to be November 2009.

Robison Ranch Cellars
2626 Robison Ranch Rd.
Walla Walla, WA 99362
509-301-3480

This winery is bonded in the state of Washington.

Rulo Winery (2000)
3525 Pranger Rd.
Walla Walla, WA 99362
509-525-7856
www.rulowinery.com

Kurt and Vicki Schlicker are owners of Rulo Winery which specializes in Viognier, Chardonnay and Syrah. The name Rulo is adopted from a grain elevator about 13 miles from Walla Walla, which was near a wheat ranch Kurt visited as a child. The winery sits on a 5.75 acre parcel of land.

Russell Creek Winery (1998)
301 Aeronca (airport)
Walla Walla, WA 99362
509-386-4401
www.russellcreek-winery.com

The winery was established in 1988 on a farm in the foothills of the Blue Mountains by Larry Krivoshein. The original home label was called "Diggers" which showed a shovel stuck in the ground near Walla Walla with flags from the Soviet Union, Canada and the United States flying across the top. The original winepress sits in the corner of his office. The small carboys he originally used to produce wine are now used to top off his current productions.

Sapolil Cellars (2002)
15 E. Main St.
Walla Walla, WA 99362
509-520-5258
www.sapolilcellars.com

Sapolil was a Native American who helped Dr. Baker build the railroad in the 1800s. To honor him the railway station was named Sapolil. The winery is built in the shadows of that landmark. Winemaker Bill Schwerin's Walla Walla heritage goes back to his grandfather, who traversed the Blue Mountains herding wild horses in a region known as Horse Heaven Hills. Bill's daughter, Abigail Schwerin, helps Sapolil produce Cabernet Sauvignon, Syrah and

Chardonnay. Their house band, Papa Loves Mambo, often plays jazz at their downtown tasting room on Friday nights.

Sapphire Mountains Cellars (2003)
883 Biscuit Ridge Rd.
Dixie, WA 99329
509-522-0961

The winery is located on forty-five acres near Dixie, WA. Raymond Monk Ph.D. is the winemaker. Their first releases included Cabernet Sauvignon, Chardonnay, Merlot and Syrah.

Saviah Cellars (2000)
1979 JB George Rd.
Walla Walla, WA 99362
509-520-5166
www.saviahcellars.com

Founded in 2000, the winery's first vintage was only 300 cases. Today the winery produces approximately 5500 cases of wine per year. Winemaker Richard Funk and his wife, Anita, both natives of Montana, moved to Walla Walla in 1991. The name Saviah is a family name for Anita's great-grandmother, a schoolteacher, artist and author, who settled in western Montana in the early 1900s. Saviah produces Chardonnay, Cabernet Sauvignon and Syrah.

Schafer Winery
178 Vineyard Ln.
Walla Walla, WA 99362

See: àMaurice winery. Anna Schafer is winemaker and partner for àMaurice.

Silver Owl Winery
1509 Beet Rd.
Walla Walla, WA 99362

Silver Owl is a bonded winery in Washington State.

Skylite Cellars (2001)
25 Campbell Rd.
Walla Walla, WA 99362
509-529-8000
www.skylitecellars.com

The downtown Walla Walla tasting room is located in the historic 1908 Quinn building and also houses the Skylite Gallery offering an array of art and artifacts collected by owners Tom and Cheryl Hodgins. Robert Smasne is the winemaker and consultant. Skylight produces Chardonnay, the NEA, Syrah, Merlot and Cabernet Sauvignon. Check out the history of Hiney Wine on their website and get a glimpse of "Lily" and "Kobe" their dogs. Tom and Cheryl Hodgins are also partners in Ash Hollow vineyard.

Sleight of Hand Cellars (2007)
16 N. Second Ave.
Walla Walla, WA 99362
509-525-3661
www.sofhcellars.com

Launched in 2007 by winemaker Trey Busch (Basel Cellars) Sleight of Hand has released "The Magician" (100% Gewurztraminer), a multi-vintage wine called "The Spellbinder" (42% Cabernet Franc, 29% Sangiovese, 29% Cabernet Sauvignon), and a "Right Bank" Bordeaux style blend called "The Archimage" (46% Merlot, 20% Cabernet Franc, 26% Cabernet Sauvignon and 1% Petit Verdot). Sleight of Hand cellars will release "The Illusionist" in the fall of 2009.

Spring Valley Vineyard (1999)
18 N. Second Ave.
Walla Walla, WA 99362
509-525-1506
www.springvalleyvineyard.com

Spring Valley Vineyard is in the middle of the wheat fields twelve miles northeast of Walla Walla. (They have a new tasting room in downtown Walla Walla). The Corkrum family heritage in the Walla Walla Valley goes back to the 1800s. The first exploration into the wine industry was planting a two acre block of Merlot in 1993. The first wine was a blend of Bordeaux varietals and was called "Uriah." In 2004, two events changed the course of the winery. Devin Derby, winemaker, died in an automobile accident. (There is a commemorative wine made by several Walla Walla wineries in his honor.) Ste Michelle Wine Estates purchased Spring Valley Vineyard winery from the Corkrum family in 2004. Mary Derby (Devin's wife and co-winemaker) has recently started another wine venture (DaMa).

Stella Fino Winery (2005)
50051 Stateline Rd.
Milton-Freewater, OR 97862
541-938-5179
www.stellafino.com

Stella Fino specializes in Italian varietals. They make a 100% Sangiovese from Pepper Bridge Vineyard and are growing Sangiovese, Nebbiolo and Barbera varietals on their 35 acre vineyard. The winery is named after Matt Steiner's (owner-winemaker) great-grandmother. Matt and his wife, Marlene, are from the East Coast. They went to school at Fairfield University in Connecticut.

Another Mystery Solved

by Pat McVay

Stephenson Cellars (2001)
755 B St. (airport)
Walla Walla, WA 99362
509-529-8200
www.stephensoncellars.com

David Stephenson is the winemaker-owner. Stephenson Cellars produces a Syrah, Merlot, Viognier and Cabernet Sauvignon. David also does lab analysis for several wineries as well as consults with new wineries.

Sulei Cellars
1509 Beet Rd.
Walla Walla, WA 99362

Sulei Cellars a bonded winery in Washington State

Sweet Valley Wines (2004)
7 W. Poplar St.
Walla Walla, WA 99362
509-526-0002
www.sweetvalleywines.com

Established in 2004, Sweet Valley Wines is Washington State's 500th winery. Four families own Sweet Valley Wines – Laura Schilling, David and Karen McDaniels, Shane and Dawn Fischer, and Kevin and Heather DeFord. David and Karen's son, Josh McDaniels, is the winemaker. In 2009 the winery will be housed in the old Walla Walla Ice Plant. Sweet Valley produces Merlot, Syrah and Viognier.

Syzygy (2002)
405 E. Boeing Ave. (airport)
Walla Walla, WA 99362
509-522-0484
www.syzygywines.com

Syzygy (pronounced "szz-eh-jee") is the moment of perfect alignment between three celestial bodies, such as that occurring during a total solar eclipse. Zach Brettler is the owner-winemaker of Syzygy.

Syzygy moved from their World War Two reclamation building at the Walla Walla airport to their new facility at the Walla Walla airport in 2005. Syzygy produces Cabernet Sauvignon and Syrah. Their "Saros" wine is a blend of Tempranillo, Malbec and Cabernet Sauvignon.

Tamarack Cellars (1998)
700 C St. (airport)
Walla Walla, WA 99362
509-526-3533
www.tamarackcellars.com

Founded in 1998 by Ron and Jamie Coleman, the winery is located in a restored World War Two fire station and barracks at the Walla Walla Airport Complex. Ron Coleman serves as winemaker and general manager. He comes to the job after a long career in the wine industry with experience in wholesale and retail sales, as a sommelier and through cellar work for Waterbrook and Canoe Ridge Wineries.

Tertulia Cellars (2005)
1564 Whitely Rd.
Walla Walla, WA 99362
509-525-5700
www.tertuliacellars.com

Tertulia is a Spanish word meaning "a social gathering of friends." Ryan Raber, winemaker, is a sixth generation Washingtonian. Ryan started out in 2001 giving tours and conducting tastings for Chateau Ste Michelle. A year later he began working in the cellar at Columbia Crest winery. In 2005 he graduated from the Center for enology and Viticulture at Walla Walla Community College. Jim O'Connell is the managing partner. Tertulia produces Merlot, Cabernet Sauvignon, Viognier and Syrah.

Terranova Cellars
3471 Pranger Rd.
Walla Walla, WA 99362

Terranova Cellars is bonded in the state of Washington. Same address as Isenhower Winery.

Thirsty Pagans (2005)
1111 Blalock Dr.
Walla Walla, WA 99326
509-301-6617
www.thirstypagans.com

Rob Chowanietz, Crandall Kyle and Jeanie Inglis-Chowanietz are the owners of Thirsty Pagans. Rob worked with John Abbott when he was at Canoe Ridge Vineyard, Jeanie worked at Waterbrook Winery and as PR director for Cayuse and Crandall worked in the office at L'Ecole No. 41. Thirsty Pagan's first release was Communion Red, a blend of Bordeaux red grapes.

TL Cellars (2004)
4122 Power Line Rd.
Walla Walla, WA 99362
509-301-3896
www.tlcellars.com

Troy and Kathy Ledwick started TL Cellars in 2004. Troy is also the winemaker for Hence Cellars. They make a Cabernet Sauvignon called Release No. One. The wine was aged in barrel for thirty-nine months. Only forty-seven cases were produced and they are individually marked.

Three Rivers Winery (1999)
5641 W. Hwy. 12
Walla Walla, WA 99362
509-526-9463
www.threeriverswinery.com

Three Rivers winery is named for the three rivers in the two appellations where its vineyard sources are located – The Columbia, Snake and Walla Walla rivers.

The owners are Steve Ahler, Bud Stocking and Duane Wollmuth. Holly Turner is the winemaker, taking over after three years as assistant winemaker. She has a bachelor's degree in biology from Western Oregon State College and extended course work at University of California at Davis. Holly also worked at Chateau Ste Michelle's

Ridge Winery and Bodega la Rural winery in Mendoza, Argentina.

The winery has a 14,000 square foot barrel room. It is set atop a knoll overlooking the surrounding vineyards, Mill Creek, the Blue Mountains and the nearby Whitman Mission. In addition, the winery features three short holes of golf for winery guests. In the spring of 2008 Foley Wine Group, a California based wine company, purchased sixty percent of Three Rivers Winery.

Trio Vintners (2004)
596 Piper Ave. (airport)
Walla Walla, WA 99362
509-529-8746
www.triovintners.com

Trio Vintners is a partnership between three Walla Walla winemakers – Tim Boushey, Denise Slattery and Steve Michener. Each brings a unique perspective and skill set to the winemaking process, and they are pooling their collective talents to create food-friendly wines from small lot production using grapes grown throughout Eastern Washington. Their winery and tasting room is located in one of the incubator wineries at the Walla Walla regional airport.

Tru Cellars (2009)
1007 W Rose St.
Walla Walla, WA 99362

Tru Cellars was bonded in March of 2009.

Trust Cellars (2005)
1050 Merlot Dr.
Walla Walla, WA 99362
509-529-4511

Steve Brooks is a former television producer at CNN. Steve worked at several wineries including Long Shadows. Brooks is the owner/winemaker of Trust Cellars. Trust Cellars produces a Syrah, rose of Cabernet Franc and a Semillon ice wine.

Tulpen Cellars (2005)
1102 Dell Ave.
Walla Walla, WA 99362
www.tulpencellars.com

Ken Hart and Rick Trumbull are the owners of Tulpen Cellars. They make their wines at Artifex.

Tytonidae Cellars (2005)
2580 Cottonwood Rd.
Walla Walla, WA 99362
509-301-8834
www.tytonidaecellars.com

Poet Katrina Roberts and her husband, Jeremy Barker, are owner-winemakers of Tytonidae Cellars. The name comes from the sub-family name of Barn Owls (tytonidae or Tyto owls). The heart shaped face is one of the main characteristics of the Barn Owl. Jeremy and Katrina's wines include a "Flying Matador Noble Red" made from 50% Tempranillo and 50% Merlot, "Gothic Roof Red" and "Gambrel Roof Red" as well as a Merlot Ice Wine.

Va Piano Vineyards (2005)
1793 JB George Rd.
Walla Walla, WA 99362
509-529-0900
www.vapianovineyards.com

Justin and Liz Wylie planted Va Piano Vineyards in 1999 with the vision of making small lots of well-balanced, full bodied reds that showcase Walla Walla's exceptional fruit along with creating a unique and familial atmosphere. In 2004 they built their Tuscan style tasting room and wine studio – offering workspace to six boutique wineries.

Vierra Vineyards (2003)
426 N. Second
Suite P
Walla Walla, WA 99362

Vierra Vineyards is a sister winery of Basel Cellars. The Vierra Vineyards tasting room is located inside the old train depot. Beginning in 2003, all of the Vierra Vineyard's wines were produced at Basel Cellars winery.

Walla Walla Vintners (1995)
225 Vineyard Ln.
Walla Walla, WA 99362
509-525-4724
www.wallawallavintners.com

Walla Walla Vintners was bonded in 1995 by winemaker-owners Myles Anderson and Gordon Venneri. They helped develop the Institute of Enology and Viticulture by donating the use of the winery during the early years of the institute. Bill von Metzger, a graduate of the Institute, is a co-winemaker. Gordon is a CPA and retired field agent for Knight of Columbus insurance and Myles was a teaching psychologist at the local community college and a founding director of the Walla Walla Institute of Enology and Viticulture. The new winery, designed and built by Alan Jones, is located off Mill Creek Road on seventeen acres near the Blue Mountains.

In 2010 they expect their estate vineyard to be in full production. It will include clones of Brunello and Sangiovese grapes, Petit Verdot as well as Merlot, Cabernet Sauvignon and Syrah. To help put the Walla Walla wine industry in perspective: in 1995 Walla Walla Vintners was the eighth bonded winery in the Walla Walla AVA. Myles and Gordon have been instrumental in bringing along the academic and hands on approach to learning about wine.

Walla Walla Village Winery (2003)
107 S. Third Ave.
Walla Walla, WA 99362
509-525-9463
www.wallawallavillagewinery.com

Barb and Lynn Irish Clark are the owners of Walla Walla Village Winery. Their son, Joel Clark, is the winemaker. The tasting room is located in a renovated 1900s building. The website has BBQ recipes and a history of their label artist, Stanley Mouse, who created album covers for The Grateful Dead, Steve Miller Band and Journey and posters for Jimi Hendrix, Cream, Frank Zappa and Janis Joplin. They make a Chardonnay, Riesling, as well as a Cabernet Franc, Merlot and Cabernet Sauvignon blend called "Bordello Red."

Walla Walla Wine Depot
315 N. Second Ave.
Walla Walla, WA 99362
509-525-5664

Walla Walla Wine Depot is a Washington bonded winery.

Walla Walla Wine Works (2008)
Highway 12 and McDonald Rd.
Walla Walla, WA 99362
www.preceptbrands.com

Seattle based Precept Wine Brands has opened a new project in Walla Walla. They will make 250,000 cases under several different brands including Pendulum Winery, Shimmer wines, Waterbrook and the Magnificent Wine Company's "The Originals" and "House Wine" labels. Precept owns twelve Washington wine brands and several import brands. The Walla Walla Valley was producing between 400,000 and 500,000 cases of wine prior to Precept's foray into the market. Precept projects it will produce up to 250,000 cases of wine which is about eight times more than the largest winery currently in Walla Walla, Canoe Ridge. As a negociant company it appears that much of Precept's wine will be made from sources outside of the Walla Walla AVA.

Washington Vintners
511 N. Second Ave.
Walla Walla, WA 99362
509-525-9532

A bonded winery in the state of Washington.

Waterbrook Winery (1984)

Sold to Precept

Waterbrook Winery was the fourth oldest in the Walla Walla Valley. It was founded in 1984 by Eric and Janet Rindal. The original winery was a converted asparagus storage facility. The name "was chosen to complement the translation from Nez Perce Indian dialect for the name Walla Walla, meaning running water." (Quote from Waterbrook website.) John Freeman is the current winemaker.

Watermill Winery (2005)
235 E. Broadway
Milton-Freewater, OR 97862
541-938-5575
www.watermillwinery.com

Earl and Lorraine Brown settled in the Walla Walla Valley in 1957 and planted their first apple orchard. It was their vision to produce and sell the finest quality fruit in the Valley. Three generations later the Brown family continues that tradition by growing premium wine grapes in the Walla Walla Valley. In 2005 the family established Watermill Winery. The winery is located in the Watermill Building in downtown Milton-Freewater, OR. The winery belongs to several environmental organizations and practices sustainable farming. They are members of Oregon LIVE, Salmon Safe and Vinea. Rich Funk of Saviah Cellars oversees the winemaking operations. You can also taste Blue Mountain Cider at the tasting room.

Waters Winery (2005)
1825 JB George Rd.
Walla Walla, WA 99362
509-525-1590
www.waterswinery.com

This new sustainable winery was founded by fifth-generation Walla Wallan Jason D. Huntley. The winemaker is Jamie Brown. They strive to produce "old world" style wines that showcase the unique terroir of the Walla Walla Valley. Jason Huntley is the founder and managing partner. Waters produces Syrah, Cabernet Sauvignon and Viognier.

Wines of Substance (2006)
1825 JB George Rd.
Walla Walla, WA 99362
509-526-6965
www.winesofsubstance.com

The website is a state of art concept. Click on an "element" and the wine's label pops into view; click for more varietal information and tasting notes of each wine. The large portfolio of Columbia Valley sourced wines goes from eclectic Counoise to Cabernet Sauvignon. The owners are Jamie Brown, Jason Huntley and Greg Harrington. The owner-winemaker, Jamie Brown, worked for Glen Fiona, Dunham Cellars and Pepper Bridge before becoming wine maker at James Leigh Cellars in 2001.

Whitman Cellars (1998)
1015 W. Pine St.
Walla Walla, WA 99362
509-529-1142
www.whitmancellars.com

The winery was started by John Edwards and Larry & Sally Thomason. The first wines were produced at Whitman cellars in 1998 and the tasting room was opened in 2001 in downtown Walla Walla. In 2002 Steve Lessard became winemaker and Whitman Cellars member. Whitman Cellars sources grapes from Walla Walla Valley and Red

Mountain appellation vineyards. The winery uses a combination of French, Hungarian and American oak barrels.

Wheat Ridge
254 Wheat Ridge Ln.
Walla Walla, WA 99362
509-301-1181

Wheat Ridge Lane is a bonded Washington winery.

Windrush Cellars
2840 Melrose St
Bldg A
Walla Walla, WA 99362

Windrush Cellars is a bonded Washington winery.

Yellow Hawk Cellar (1998)
343 S. Second Ave.
Walla Walla, WA 99362
509-529-1714
www.yellowhawkcellar.com

Yellow Hawk Cellar began production in 1998 with its first releases in 2000. The owner-winemaker, Tim Sampson, and his wife, Barbara Hetrick came to Walla Walla in 1995. Tim worked at Canoe Ridge until 2000 when he became cellar master at Seven Hills Winery. The winery specializes in Italian varietals – Sangiovese, Barbera, Muscat Canelli, and Orange Muscat. The winery is named after the creek, which is likely named after the legendary Indian chief, Peu-Peu Mox-Mox, who was known as "Yellow Bird." There is no Yellow Hawk roaming the area but there are pair of Swanson Hawks that nest in the nearby Creek.

Zerba Cellars (2002)
85530 Highway 11
Milton-Freewater, OR 97862
541-938-9463
www.zerbacellars.com

Zerba Cellars is a family owned, estate winery located in the heart of the Walla Walla Valley appellation. The estate vineyards are planted in the Walla Walla Valley's viticultural zones. Zerba also purchases small lots of premium wine grapes from select vineyards in Oregon and Washington. Zerba produces a Chardonnay, Cabernet Sauvignon, Merlot, Syrah and Sangiovese.

"I will fight no more, forever." Chief Joseph

The Nez Perce were the largest ethnic group in the Columbia Plateau. They acquired horses in the mid 1700's and became known for their outstanding horsemanship. In 1877 Chief Joseph was forced to retreat from his ancestral homeland of the Wallowa Valley. The band traveled almost 1800 miles with the U.S. Army in pursuit in what is considered one of the most brilliant military retreats in American history. Their travels covered much of the land that is now part of the Walla Walla Valley appellation. They were finally captured in Montana, just 30 miles from the Canadian border. Chief Joseph addressed his tribe, "Hear me, my chiefs. I am tired; my heart is sick and sad. From where the sun now stands I will fight no more, forever."

Walla Walla Part III

THE CEMETERY

In Roslyn, Washington (where Northern Exposure was filmed, this has nothing to do with the television series but it might help in your Monday evening trivia games) the cemetery is segmented by lodges and by country of origin making twenty-five plus areas within the cemetery. They provide a unique perspective into the history of that small town (population about 1000). We also feel that those wineries (and restaurants later on) that were part of the history of an area provide a window into how the wine and food industry developed. In some ways it is, "Do you remember ...." time, in other ways it reminds you of the exhilaration of success and failure. The cemetery pays homage to those who were ahead of their time, and a reminder to those who want to venture into the expanding wine and food world that their dreams are going to meet some obstacles.

Biscuit Ridge (1987)
Dayton, WA

Biscuit Ridge winery was started by Jack and Helen Durham. The primary wine was a dry Gewürztraminer. Jack died in 1991, and his wife, Helen, died in 1997. In 1998, Duane and Mary Wollmuth began reconstructing the vineyard. In 1999, they became involved in the Three River Winery project and planted some Cabernet Franc.

Bunchgrass Winery (1997)   ALERT!!
Highway 12
Walla Walla, WA 99362
www.bunchgrasswinery.com

Roger Cockerline housed Bunchgrass Winery in a former dairy barn located on the family farm. He concentrated on making limited quantities of Bordeaux style blends and Cabernet Sauvignon aged in American and French oak. The last commercial vintage made by Bunchgrass was its 2005. Just as we were going to print we heard that Bunchgrass is rising from the compost pile and is being revived by Bill vonMetzger, Cockerline, Tom Olander and Barb Commare.

Colvin Vineyards (1999)
1011 Abbott Rd.
Walla Walla, WA 99362

Colvin Vineyards was a family owned winery housed in a log and stone structure. The focus of Mark and JoAnne Colvin, co-owners, was ultra premium red wines including Cabernet Sauvignon, Merlot, Syrah, Cabernet Franc and Carmenere. The winery was closed in 2008. Jancis Robinson, a British wine writer, singled out Colvin's Carmenere (Grand Vidure) as one of the best examples of the wine she had tasted.

Flying B Vineyards

Drew Bledsoe owns the vineyard and was reported to be considering using the name for his wine (named after his grandfather's former cattle ranch in Ellensburg) and having it made at Artifex Wine Company. (Source *Walla Walla Grape Vine* Nov 15, 2007) We can't tell if this winery name has one foot in the grave, or out of the grave.

Washington Wine Country Fact Eight

Lewis and Clark entered the Walla Walla area for the first time in October of 1805 about twelve miles from the junction of the Snake and Columbia rivers. A few days later the Corps of Engineers reached the Columbia and Meriwether Lewis showed off his great eyesight by proclaiming, "Ocian in view! O, the joy!" After more than a month later and several delays The Corps reached the Pacific Ocean. A year later The Corps returned to the Walla Walla area, their route taking them through the present day towns of Waitsburg, Pomeroy and Dayton reaching the Snake River in May.

Part IV

Vineyards of the Walla Walla Valley

Walla Walla Valley became an American Viticultural Area (AVA) in 1984. From its humble beginnings in the 1970s with about sixty acres of vineyards and four wineries it is now home to more than a hundred wineries and more than fifteen hundred acres of vineyards. The following are some of the vineyards in the area. They produce grapes for their own winery as well as grapes for many other wineries. We have tried to highlight some of the different types of vineyards in the area. You can not have great wine without having great vineyards. The vineyards have caretakers who use their knowledge of the climate, soil and idiosyncrasies of the vineyard to produce the great wines of the Walla Walla Valley.

Ahler is owned and operated by Three Rivers Winery partners Steve and Ann Ahler. This vineyard is located northeast of Walla Walla. The first crops of Cabernet Sauvignon and Syrah from this vineyard were harvested in 2001.

Alderbanks is one of the oldest vineyards in the area. They often have very low production and are in an early ripening site in the Walla Walla Valley.

Armada was planted in 2001 by Christophe Baron of Cayuse. Armada contains several Rhone varietals including Grenache, Syrah and Mourvedre. With four feet between vines and five feet between rows, 2178 vines were planted per acre – nearly double the standard vine quantity – and easily marks it as one of the highest density vineyards in the Walla Walla Valley. It is biodynamically farmed.

Ash Hollow is located in the west end of the valley. It has a southern exposure with panoramic views. The vineyards received six to eight inches of rainfall per year. There are thirty-nine acres of Cabernet Sauvignon, Merlot and Syrah vines.

Biscuit Ridge was planted in the mid-1980s by Jack and Helen Durham. This vineyard is currently owned and operated by

Duane and Mary Wollmuth. The vineyard is located in the far northeastern corner of the appellation. Unlike most other vineyards in the valley which lie at an elevation of 1100 to 1300 feet and consist of Bordeaux and Rhone varietals, Biscuit Ridge lies at roughly 1800 feet and is most conducive to cold hardy varietals such as Gewurztraminer and Cabernet Franc.

Braden View (renamed Sconni Block) vineyard enjoys southern exposure and a gradual sloping landscape. Five acres of certified Cabernet Sauvignon grapes and four acres of certified Merlot grapes were planted in the spring of 2000. Additional rows are being added to the vineyard. The grape rows have a north/south orientation, allowing fruit to absorb Walla Walla's sun rays throughout the long growing season. The vertical trellis system also maximizes sun exposure, enhances fruit quality and simplifies the harvest. The irrigation system begins with an 800 foot deep well accessing the basalt aquifer. Water is delivered to each grape plant as needed through a modern, above ground, drip irrigation system.

Buckley Terrace has a steep, south facing slope. Buckley Terrace reminds you of the famous cornas region in the Northern Rhone Valley of France, renowned for its production of Syrah. Planted at a spacing of 10x2 the dense plantings promise to yield a wine that is muscular, rich and complex. For frost protection an overhead sprinkler system has been installed.

Cailloux (plural for 'stone' in French) is a Cayuse vineyard. They planted ten acres of grapes in 1996 along the ancient cobblestone riverbed of the Walla Walla Valley.

Cougar Hills was planted with cuttings from Windrow Vineyard (the original Seven Hills Vineyard) and Cailloux Vineyard. Cougar Crest Winery currently farms Syrah, Cabernet Sauvignon, Merlot, Cabernet Franc, Viognier, Petit Verdot and Malbec at the vineyard.

Double River Ranch is a thirty-three acre vineyard located on the west side of Highway Nine as you head south towards Oregon. The site was established in the spring of 2000 and is planted in Bordeaux varietals. It sits at an elevation of 900 feet and has many microclimates on the property due to differences in sun exposures, wind and soil composition. A million gallon pond was established to provide enough water for irrigating the vineyards. The VSP trellis system is used at Double River.

Flying B is owned by Doubleback Winery owner Drew Bledsoe. (Note – he also owns and is developing McQueen Vineyard.)

Frenchtown is named after the French fur trappers of the mid-1800s that once populated the area. The site is dedicated to red wine grapes and slopes to the north, much like Seven Hills Vineyard. It is planted on deep sandy loam and uses drip irrigation to manage the water supply.

Heather Hill was established in the spring of 2001. Heather Hill vineyard is located in Oregon, just east of Seven Hills Vineyard. Terraces were installed at this site because of the steep terrain.

Leonetti Estate is the oldest vineyard in the Walla Walla Valley. It was planted by Gary Figgins in 1974. The small lots of grapes (A half acre each of Merlot and Syrah used to blend with the Leonetti Sangiovese and one acre of Cabernet Franc) surround the winery. The grapes are dry land farmed on Hermiston silt loam.

Les Collines is located in the foothills of the Blue Mountains at 1200 feet. Designed and built by Norm McKibben and his son, Shane McKibben, Les Collines is one of most technologically advanced vineyard in Washington State. The first fifty acres were planted in 2001. Norm and his partner, Michael Murr, have plans to expand the vineyard to 250 acres which would make it one of the largest in the Walla Walla Valley.

The vines are all vertically trained and drip irrigated. The wireless irrigation system is computer controlled and fed by a 1,400 foot deep well that feeds into a three million gallon pond. Weather is monitored and updated every fifteen minutes on the www.lescollines.com website. The grapes can be hand picked or machine harvested with the only Pellanc "over-the-row" machine in the state, which is also used for spraying and pre-pruning.

The soils consist of a deep silt loam. The vineyard is researching and working towards sustainable viticulture through soil biology and chemical alternatives, such as compost and compost tea with water-run food sources for the organisms.

Loess was planted in 2002. Leonetti's Loess vineyard is located on the hillside next to the winery. It is sustainably farmed under the protocols of VINEA.

Mill Creek Upland was planted in 1997. Leonetti's Mill Creek Upland vineyard is planted on a 10% southern exposed slope. This vineyard has a unique mesoclimate. Every night shortly after dusk there is rapid temperature drop of between 25-40 degrees from the daytime highs. This results in the maturing berries developing very dark color, intense fruit flavors and excellent acid retention. It is sustainably farmed under the protocols of VINEA.

Morrison Lane is the oldest Syrah vineyard in the Valley and primary source of Syrah grapes for Morrison Lane Vineyard. They also produce small quantities of Sangiovese, Counoise, Mourvedre, Carmenere and Viognier.

Pepper Bridge was planted in 1991 and has since expanded to a total of 169 acres of wine grapes. Pepper Bridge Vineyard grapes are known throughout the state of Washington for their outstanding quality and are featured in many of the premium wines produced in the Walla Walla Valley. The vineyard employs cutting-edge technology for its weather and irrigation systems. Over 60 moisture-measuring points are spread throughout the farm and moisture data is logged once an hour, 24 hours a day. Weather data such as temperature, humidity, wind and energy units are linked into the computer system and recorded around the clock.

Tom Waliser has been the vineyard manager at Pepper Bridge Vineyard since its beginnings in 1991. All grapes are grown on split canopy trellises, in which the vines are trained both up and down off the cordon, or grape-bearing wire. All grapes are on the Smart-Dyson trellis system except five acres of Merlot, which are on the Scott-Henry trellis system. The soils in this vineyard are Walla Walla silt loam, which are wind-blown glacial loess that are young and full of minerals. This silt loam contains one-third sand and is very free draining.

River Rock vineyard was planted in 2000 by the Dibble family. They planted Cabernet Sauvignon in a very warm and rocky area in Milton-Freewater, Oregon. Dana Dibble is the king of fruit production in Middleton-Freewater. His farm has cherries, apricots and apples. In addition, he grows Cabernet Sauvignon, Syrah and Viognier for several Walla Walla wineries.

Seven Hills East is managed by Chris Banek. Seven Hills Vineyard is situated just ten miles south of Pepper Bridge Winery on the edge of the Walla Walla appellation.

The original plantings date back to 1981 and have expanded to almost 200 acres of premium wine grapes. Seven Hills Vineyard is the source of fruit for many of the fine wineries in the state and valley.

During the first months of each growing season irrigation is pulled from the Hudson Bay ditch. After ditch water is shut off to protect the fish, irrigation switches to a deep basalt well, which is drilled over 1100 feet through hard rock. Water is distributed from a surge pond to the grapes through both above ground and buried drip lines that can also spread required fertilization with the water. Grapes are one of the most efficient crops, in terms of water requirement, and the drip system of irrigation eliminates wasted water. The moisture monitoring system alerts the vineyard managers any time moisture gets below the root zone of the vines. This allows the vineyard to irrigate only as much water as will be taken up by the plants and eliminates contamination of the groundwater system. With the exception of five acres of Geneva Double Curtain all grapes are grown on the Smart-Dyson split canopy trellises, in which the vines are trained both up and down off the cordon, or grape-bearing wire. The soils in this vineyard are Ellingoford silt loam, which are windblown glacial loess that is geologically very young and full of minerals. The other side of the grain elevators is Seven Hills West, managed by Tom Waliser.

Seven Hills West was planted in the early 1980s by the McClellan family. The Cabernet Sauvignon grown down in the lake bed stones of Seven Hills West is quite different than the Cabernet Sauvignon grown in the newer and hillier Seven Hills East. Often the same fruit is picked two weeks later in Seven Hills West than the same grapes in Seven Hills East. Since 1994 it has been managed by Tom Waliser (who also manages Pepper Bridge Vineyard, and has his own winery, Beresan).

Spofford Station vineyard lies a stone's throw south of the Oregon-Washington line, nestled in the windshed of the Blue Mountains. Spofford Station is a millennium vineyard with hundreds of years of history behind it. For generations the land was used for wheat and pea rotations which created a rich and fertile soil.

Spring Valley is situated twelve miles northeast of Walla Walla. Spring Valley vineyard rests amid the picturesque hills of wheat in southeastern Washington State. Extensive evaluation of the terroir illustrates a mesoclimate ideally suited for growing wine grapes. Further examination revealed separate microclimates that would allow individual blocks of vines to develop their own distinct characteristics. The initial two acre block of Merlot was planted in 1993. Placed on a south-southwest facing hillside, the vines follow the North-South slope of the hills in vertical rows. This orientation, coupled with the slope of the vineyard affords the vines optimal use of sunshine, drainage and the reflective nature of the surrounding hills. Today Spring Valley vineyard is planted in more than forty acres of red varietals

Stellar is a ten acre estate vineyard and was planted in 1997 in a warm antediluvian riverbed. Otis Kenyon Wine and Stephenson Cellars purchased Stellar vineyard in the fall of 2006.

Va Piano vineyards were planted in 1999 by Justin and Liz Wylie. In December of 2005, Va Piano celebrated their grand opening by releasing their first vintages, a 2003 Cabernet Sauvignon and eight 2003 Syrah.

Vista Montagna is a tiny Cabernet Franc vineyard located on the eastern end of Walla Walla. Vista Montagna ("Mountain View" in Italian) sits on a bench overlooking Walla Walla. This unique location is above the cold air pockets that challenge vineyards in lower locations. The vineyard is able to hang grapes on the vine for longer than other vineyards in the area because the fall frosts do not reach this vineyard until November. The soil is the loam that the many floods over the centuries have deposited in the Walla Walla Valley.

Windrow was originally planted as a part of Seven Hills Vineyard and renamed Windrow in 1995. The 33 acre vineyard has produced fruit for L'Ecole No. 41, Leonetti, Walla Walla Vintners and many others.

The Vines Parted

by Alexei Kazantsev

Part V

GOTTA EAT

For Sam and me a trip to any location whether it be New York, San Francisco or the Walla Walla Valley is not a complete one unless we take the time to experience the local restaurants. We have organized this section in the same twisted way we plan all of our trips. What kind of food are we looking for? Where do the locals go? Finally, if we want a special night out for food and wine where would we go? (Or another way to put it, do we need to get reservations?)

Where can we get good local food on the run? After all, we are here to taste wine. We don't want to sit around for three hours during lunch and miss out on any of the more than one hundred winery tasting rooms.

Here is our food stained road that has led us to some restaurants that offer unique food and quality. We put the ✒ symbol next to our favorite value spots and gourmet restaurants. We define these places as ones that we stop at even when we aren't hungry.

Backstage Bistro (Bistro)
230 E. Main St.
Walla Walla, WA 99362
509-526-0690

Backstage Bistro is a place for coffee in the morning with a cinnamon roll or a cheese steak sandwich for lunch or steak and seafood for dinner in the evening. You will find a long list of local wines to enjoy with your food. You might even find music going on during the weekend as well.

Brassiere Four (French)
4 East Main St.
Walla Walla, WA 99362
509-529-2011

A new restaurant is the Brassiere Four which opened in the old Grapefields location. It has a luncheon menu that features quiche, gourmet pizza and charcuterie. The salads have locally grown produce and the coffee is from Stumptown roasters in Portland.

Creektown Café (Continental)
1129 S. Second Ave.
Walla Walla, WA 99362
509-522-4777

The Creektown is both a casual place for lunch and a gourmet dining experience. The luncheon menu features Thundering Hooves beef, Jamaican chicken burger or a garden burger. They have panini sandwiches, cumin apple crab cakes and seasonal vegetable lasagna. They now offer a mid-day menu for those who get through tasting wine at 3:00 in the afternoon and realize they forgot lunch.

The dinner menu includes crispy calamari and house cured wild salmon on their appetizer menu. For a main course you might try seared prawns and scallops, steelhead trout or roast pheasant with hedgehog mushrooms. They also feature Thundering Hooves pork and beef, Fahrenbacher Farms lamb with Gypsy Sally's arugula. They had a banana squash gnocchi the last time I was there and a seafood Caesar salad. Don't forget their bakery with local apple pastries and pies.

T Maccarone's (Italian)
4 No. Colville
Walla Walla, WA 99362
509-522-4776

Tom Maccarone is owner of this Italian restaurant. For dinner you can get a range of pasta from Arrabiata to lasagna. Dinner entrees include lamb, beef, chicken and seafood selections.

Oasis (Perry Mason)
85698 Highway 333
Milton-Freewater, OR 97862
541-938-4776

If you are in the vineyard area and don't want to go to the taco shack you could try the Oasis Restaurant which has been in operation since the 1940s The Oasis is one of those catch-all restaurants with hamburgers, steaks, prawns and prime rib. The ambiance is classic roadside. A place where Paul Drake might have stopped when he was digging up dirt for Perry Mason – in black and white, of course.

Pho Sho (Vietnamese)
123 W. Alder Street
Walla Walla, WA 99362
509-535-9794

Pho Sho is a Vietnamese noodle shop. They offer a variety of phos (soups), a selection of egg and spring rolls as well as pork, egg and vegetarian buns.

Saffron Mediterranean Kitchen (Mediterranean)
125 W. Alder St.
Walla Walla, WA 99362
509-525-2112

Saffron serves Mediterranean food with a local flair. The chef, Chris Ainsworth, received a nomination for James Beard regional chef in 2009. This is a good place for small plates (although they aren't that small) and a glass of wine. They will bring you a basket of bread (I had an olive foccacia bread on one occasion and a Moroccan flat bread on another) with a small dipping dish of olive oil and garlic cloves. During the summer they often have a gazpacho that features local vegetables.

For entrees I had their lamb tajine last time. Served in the traditional Moroccan dish (the base has the food – lamb sweet potatoes, squash, dried fruits, aromatic spices) and the top looks like a clay dunce cap. They take the dunce away and leave you with a magnificent dish.

You can often get a Kobe steak or a seafood pappardelle as well. The menu changes to reflect the availability of local, fresh ingredients.

Sweet Basil Pizzeria (Italian)
5 S. 1st Ave.
Walla Walla, WA 99362
509-529-1950

Sweet Basil Pizzeria features New York style pizza. Now I've been to New York and I still don't know what that means because if you go to Ray's it means "oily" slices or if you go to Brooklyn's Grimaldi it means the pizza (no slices served at Grimaldi's) was cooked in a coal oven. So I'm not sure which pizza establishment Sweet Basil has in mind but I will say that the pizzas are innovative and have a good crust. (That's about all that matters to me.) Sweet Basil offers a selection of local wines with their food and don't be surprised if they take advantage of local, in-season vegetables and herbs for their pizza toppings.

A Taco Shack (Mexican)

Next to a tienda, next to the Oasis at 85698 Highway 339

If you are in the country looking at the vineyards, go about six miles south of Walla Walla to a place I call the Taco Shack. It is a small eatery attached to a grocery store which serves tacos, burritos and sweet tamales, located west of Highway 12 on Stateline Road.

Taco Wagon

When it is parked, Sixth and Main

I think this is my favorite taco wagon in the region. Besides the usual suspects of pork, chicken, beef and vegetable tacos you can get lengua and cabeza. For you taco fanatics you know what I mean. They have two types of sauces and will add on sour cream and avocado.

Taqueria Yungapeti (Mexican)
320 S. Ninth Ave.
Walla Walla, WA 99362
509-526-9494

Taqueria Yungapeti is a converted drive-in; Yungapeti is more spacious than the taco wagon or shack (i.e. there is room for a group of people to sit down). They specialize in tacos and burritos and their condiment bar includes a choice of hot sauces and pickled vegetables (think hot peppers and carrots). It has all of the atmosphere of a taco wagon but you can get out of the rain if need be. It also is a bit friendlier to the vegetarian-seeking-taco-wagon-aficionado.

Walla Walla Worm Ranch (Mexican and Bait)
1186 Wallula Ave.
Walla Walla, WA 99362
509-529-3629

One of our favorite taco burrito holes-in-the-wall is the Walla Walla Worm Ranch. In addition to authentic Mexican food they can satisfy all of our bait and tackle requirements. It is comforting to sit down and eat your carnitos taco while you look around the walls and see if there is anything you forgot for your upcoming fishing trip like nets, worms or flies.

Winter in the Vineyard

By Alexei Kazantsev

Walla Walla – A Special Occasion

Gourmet Food, Atmosphere, Wine
(and most of the patrons in long pants)

The Marc Restaurant (continental)

6 West Rose St.
Walla Walla, WA 99362
509-525-2200

The Marc is located in the Marcus Whitman Hotel. It is a grand hotel with spacious lobby, elegant dining room. For lunch you can get a clam chowder or potato leek soup. The Marc has several salads, traditional sandwiches (burger, club, Reuben) fish tacos and barbecue chicken wrap. The dinner menu has a selection of appetizers including beef steak tataki, fried calamari, beet salad and an ahi skewer.

The Marc is one of those classic dining rooms where you can still get a tableside Caesar salad for two (using Happy Free Girl Eggs from the Monteillet Fromagerie). They have a number of flat bread appetizers including house-made Italian sausage with caramelized onions, heirloom potatoes and provolone with basil pesto and a sautéed chanterelle mushroom flat bread with caramelized onions, provolone and chevre cheese. You can get a crab and prawn fettuccini for an entrée or Alaskan halibut with sautéed spinach and Meyer lemon cream. The Marc has a good wine list with a number of local wines by the glass. For something different you can call ahead and reserve the chef's table and watch your food being prepared as you dine.

Whitehouse-Crawford

55 Cherry St.
Walla Walla, WA 99362
509-525-2222

The Whitehouse-Crawford was one of the first gourmet restaurants to open up as the Walla Walla wine industry exploded. Chef Jamie Guerin has brought a wealth of experience to Walla Walla. He worked at the Mayflower Hotel in Washington, D.C. before going to Fullers in Seattle and working under Chef Monique Barbeau. He later became sous-chef at Campagne in Seattle (working with Tamara Murphy and Jim Drohman). Like many chefs in the area Chef Guerin looks to the local producers for seasonal vegetables and fruit.

Appetizers include Vietnamese style calamari, cured foie gras with hazelnuts, apple chutney and toast (we usually order this while we decide what we want to eat), Penn Cove mussels steamed with hard cider, shoulder bacon, sweet onions and cream.

Entrees include American Kobe beef steak with red wine sauce, mushrooms sautéed in foie gras butter or a house made tagliatelle pasta with exotic mushrooms, sun dried tomatoes, sherry and Parmesan Reggiano. I've had Arctic Char with fennel-celery salad and a citrus sauce "Ripert" and a roast duck with celery root remoulade, pork belly and house made applesauce.

The desserts include Irish chocolate pudding with brandied cherries and toffee crème anglaise or lemon-olive oil cake with hazelnut ice cream and blood orange sauce.

Whitehouse Crawford is open only for dinner and entrees range from twenty-five to forty dollars. It is a special place with a great wine list that emphasizes local producers, but note that you are paying for the expertise of the chef, the great ingredients and the ambiance of the 100 year old building that houses the restaurant and we believe it is worth the price.

Walla Walla -- Coffee, muffins or dessert

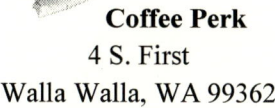

Coffee Perk
4 S. First
Walla Walla, WA 99362

Coffee Perk has pastries and a full array of coffee drinks. It is one of those low key coffee houses that make you think a real live Bohemian might walk in the front door and start reciting poetry. If Coffee Perk doesn't have the iambic pentameter you are looking for you might wander over to Merchant's.

John's Wheatland Bakery
1828 Isaacs
Walla Walla, WA 99362
509-522-2253

John's Wheatland Bakery is the place to pick up fresh baked bread (last time I had the cheese onion challah) and a few cookies. With only a hundred wineries to visit in the Walla Walla area you can drive for blocks before you hit the next winery so it is nice to have a bag of cookies to help you on your safari.

Merchant's LTD
21 East Main
Walla Walla, WA 99362
509-525-0900

Merchant's is one of the oldest establishments in town. Since 1976 they have been promoting sandwiches on great bread. The sign says French Bakery and it has been one of their trademarks. Every day you can find fresh breads, pastries, cakes, cookies, muffins and pie. You can get a latte and sit outside on the sidewalk and watch Walla Walla pass you by. They have music on selected weekends and wine by the glass.

Starbucks (downtown)
28 East Main St.
Walla Walla, WA 99362
509-525-4893

There are several Starbuck's locations in Walla Walla offering up coffee and pastries.

One of our favorite places is **Salumiere Cesario** for gourmet groceries. You can get cheeses, breads, picnic lunches, chocolates and artisanal salumi (cured meats).

Outside Walla Walla

Waitsburg

The Jimgermanbar in Waitsburg combined with the Whoopemup Hollow make this a town worth stopping in. You can get Cajun food at the Whoopemup or Etruscan tapas at Jimgermanbar.

Jimgermanbar (Etruscan!!)
119 Main St.
Waitsburg, WA 99361
509-337-6001

The owners tongue in cheek reference to Etruscan snacks (instead of tapas) made us want to stop in Waitsburg and see what was going on. It is amazing and I don't think the Palouse hills have ever had so many different food aromas waft across the wheat fields as those produced by Jimgermanbar, Whoopemup Café, Patit Creek and the Weinhard restaurant. It is a reason to take the "other way home" once in awhile. At Jimgerman bar you can get small plates. Almonds, Olives Crostini (banquerones, sweet onion, lovage pesto and Mama Lil's peppers) or prosciutto with Manchego cheese or chorizo sofrito. The menu also has organic Italian polenta with basil pesto, salt cod and potato brandade with black truffle salsa and Hudson Valley Duck leg confit with duck fat potatoes.

Whoopemup Hollow Café (Cajun)
120 Main St.
Waitsburg, WA 99361
509-337-9000

A Cajun restaurant in Waitsburg, Louisiana, maybe, but not in Waitsburg, Washington. On the other hand, what else would you want to eat if Etruscan snacks weren't at the top of your list and you were in Waitsburg? The Whoopsters have crawfish pie, Jamaican jerk shrimp and corn fritters for appetizers that is if you don't want the smoked duck breast, pan fried oysters or file gumbo with sausage and chicken. They also have po'boy sandwiches with pan-fried shrimp, oysters, catfish or buttermilk-fried chicken tenders. For dinner you can get

Bry's famous jambalaya, chicken Savannah style, cornmeal fried catfish or Whoopemup mac 'n' cheese. They will also serve you steak "Norte Americano" and seafood etouffee.

Dayton

Patit Creek Restaurant (French roadside)
725 E. Dayton Ave.
Dayton, WA 99328
509-382-2625

In Dayton is one of the most highly acclaimed restaurants in the state of Washington, Patit Creek. It is one of only two four star rated restaurants east of the Cascade Mountains by *Northwest Best Places*. I've been going to Bruce and Heather Hiebert's restaurant for twenty years and there is a good reason this French restaurant nestled at the East end of town has garnered such recognition. The restaurant's walls are covered with black and white photos of actors and actresses from the early part of the twentieth century and the paneling is a modern 1970's style.

All of the food is made from scratch. Appetizers will include items like chevre cheese stuffed dates or escargot. Entrees include classics like filet mignon poivre verte, Medallions of Beef Hiebert (can't go wrong when the chef names it after himself), lamb shank or sautéed duck breast with red wine, currant and port demi-glace. Some nights they might have lamb chops, saffron curried mussels, glazed elk medallions, shrimp scampi or coq au vin. Desserts, even if you have to get them to go, are a must because Heather bakes all of them from scratch – fruit pastries to chocolate tortes and seasonal pies. They also have a good wine list with many of the outstanding local wines.

As you drive from Walla Walla you might think you are the only one who knows about this place and aren't worried that you didn't make a reservation. You would be wrong on most days. Call ahead because those of us who have been going here for twenty years have spilled the beans, this place is worth the trip.

Weinhard Café (Continental)
258 E. Main St.
Dayton, WA 99328
509-382-4032

The Weinhard Café is part of the National Register of Historic places. The hotel was built in the late 19th century and has fifteen rooms. The lunch menu caters to locals and visitors. They have soups, salads, vegetable lasagna, vegetable samosas, panini sandwiches and pizzas. For dinner you might start with a beet avocado salad with feta and sherry vinaigrette or a bacon gorgonzola caramelized onion tart. You might get a lamb curry over jasmine rice, pork tenderloin with port sauce or baked penne pasta with goat cheese. I've also had sautéed true cod with grapefruit salsa and braised red cabbage. They will have pie (raspberry rhubarb, pecan bourbon, coconut lemon or sour cream apple with pecans) and maybe a white chocolate mousse with raspberry sauce. The menu, like Patit Creek, changes often to reflect the availability of local products.

Part VI

Ain't Gonna Eat There No More

As with any burgeoning industry you get a bit of turnover, and not always the apple or cherry kind. We cite the following as a historical perspective, not a comment on the establishment. We frequented several of these places and we just want to warn you not to get your hopes up about a former favorite.

The Food Cemetery

26 Brix – This restaurant had crab cakes, hummus and a cheese tour for appetizers. The entrees included steak, free range chicken and fish entrees. The wine list was an extensive list of Washington wines as well as some wines from around the world. Too crowded to get into when it opened up; too quiet to eat when it closed.

Grapefields -- The food here was eclectic. They had a good retail wine selection and you could choose a bottle of wine, pay a corkage fee and drink it with dinner. So, if you were having wine with dinner this made the dinner affordable but several reviews on the internet felt the dinners were overpriced. I think they forgot to consider the savings they had on a bottle of wine (or perhaps they always drank tap water only with dinner.) The cemetery is filled with restaurants with good ideas. That's better than being filled with ill-fated patrons of bad restaurants.

Luscious by Nature specialized in fresh, seasonal food and small plates. They offered to plan your wine tour and create a customized picnic for your group. Good ideas but the tourist season is short and this urban market was unable to make it.

Caravaggio – perhaps being on Terminal Loop Road was an omen. One of the first reviews I saw said "(Caravaggio) are the latest occupants of airport dining facility." Your final exam is on the following topic. Places with a history of failed occupants are the fault of the businesses, the owners of the building, food ghosts or the location's name?

Destination Grill featured steaks, smoked prime rib, stone fired gourmet pizza and seafood. They also had micro brews and fruit infused cocktails. They said they had the world's only Walla Walla Sweet Oniontini. Located at the train depot. The Depot has been the site of several restaurants. See exam question in the Caravaggio obituary.

McVay Ate Here

Part VII

GOTTA SLEEP

We have a list of places to sleep. Our main goal is to discuss wine and food but we know you will want a place to put your feet up at night to read our book. Here is a list – but as we speak someone is probably breaking ground to put up another hotel to accommodate the ever increasing population that is stomping its way to Walla Walla. We have included some links for additional resources for you to find hotels in the region.

Best Western
7 E. Oak St.
Walla Walla, WA 99362
509-525-4700

Green Gables Inn
922 Bonsella
Walla Walla, WA 99362
509-525-5501

Holiday Inn Express
1433 W. Pine St.
Walla Walla, WA 99362
509-525-6200

Howard Johnson Express
325 E. Main St.
Walla Walla, WA 99362
509-529-4360

Inn at Abeja
2014 Mill Creek Rd.
Walla Walla, WA 99362
509-522-1234

Inn at Blackberry Creek
1126 Pleasant
Walla Walla, WA 99362
509-522-5233

La Quinta
520 N. Second Ave.
Walla Walla, WA 99362
509-525-2522

Marcus Whitman
6 W. Rose St.
Walla Walla, WA 99362
509-525-2200

Super 8 Motel
2315 Eastgate St. N.
Walla Walla, WA 99362
509-525-800

Top of the Mountain
9051 Mill Creek Rd.
Walla Walla, WA 99362
509-529-528

Whitehouse-Crawford Hotel
55 Cherry St.
Walla Walla, WA 99362
509-525-2222

Washington Wine Country Fact Nine

The 2003 Vintage saw 108,000 tons of grapes harvested. Washington winemakers and wine grape growers rate the 2003 vintage as one of the best in history, particularly for red grapes. The harvest started in early September and finished in late October.

Part VIII

Walla Walla Links

www.wallawallawine.com

(A membership organization of wineries)

www.washingtonwine.org

(Represents 500 wineries & 350 growers)

www.wallawalla.org

(Walla Walla tourist site)

www.lescollines.com

(Weather station)

www.vineatrust.com

(Walla Walla valley sustainable agriculture organization)

Do you think lonely, or ice wine?

Spokane and Northern Idaho Wineries

Spokane and Northern Idaho form a long narrow corridor that stretches from Lewiston, Idaho almost two hundred miles north to Sandpoint, Idaho. Within that region Spokane is home to the majority of wineries. It is a big area that is rich in Native American history, the explorations of Lewis and Clark and the new history of the wine industry.

Spokane is the primary tourist destination spot in Eastern Washington. The city features the Lilac Festival and Torchlight Parade in May. Also in May is the Bloomsday Race which has drawn as many as 50,000 runners. Hoopfest in June gets several thousand 3 on 3 team entrees. First Night on New Year's Eve brings the downtown to life as does Artwalk, the first Friday of every month.

Local golfing features some of the top Public Courses in the country (and host to the PGA at the turn of the 20th century!). There is skiing at four major resorts in the area.

Riverfront Park hosts events throughout the year including Fourth of July celebrations. Pig Out in the Park over Labor Day weekend features cuisine from area restaurants. The remnants of the 1974 World's Fair include a park that is often used for concerts and local events as well as an IMAX theater. In the winter you can skate in the outdoor public ice skating rink.

Coeur d'Alene is situated on Coeur d'Alene Lake which attracts visitors from all over the world during the summer months. Golfing is one of the major attractions with the Coeur d'Alene Resort, Indian Canyon and Circle Raven being three of the most popular courses. The streets come alive the second Friday of each month with Artwalk and there are many festivals during the summer.

Sandpoint is home to the summer music festival and in the winter skiing is a major attraction at Sweitzer Basin.

The Lewiston and Clarkston areas feature the Snake and Clearwater rivers where Lewis and Clark explored in the early 1800s.

Part I – Wine Tour

The Wineries

Arbor Crest Wine Cellars (1982)
4705 N. Fruit Hill Rd.
Spokane, WA 99217
509-927-9463
www.arborcrest.com

Dr. Harold Mielke and Marcia Mielke started Arbor Crest winery in 1982. Scott Harris was their first winemaker. Kristina Mielke-van Loben Sels is the second generation to oversee Arbor Crest. Kristina brings both education and practical skills to her work. She graduated from the University of California at Davis as a fermentation scientist. She returned to Spokane after several years as an assistant at Ferrari-Carano Vineyards and Winery in California. Her husband, James van Loben Sels, is an experienced viticulturist.

The tasting room is located at the Royal Riblet Mansion which was built in 1924. The three story Florentine house is surrounded by an arched gatekeeper's house, sunken rose garden and open-air pagoda. You can even play chess or checkers, if you bring enough people, on the life sized checkerboard. Newton Riblet's brother, Byron, built trams for ski resorts all over the world. He installed a 450 foot tram from this estate to the river valley below. Newton was an inventor and created such devices as a pattern sprinkler system, mechanical parking garage and a square wheel tractor (on display at the winery).

The winery produces Sauvignon Blanc, Riesling, Chardonnay, Merlot, Cabernet Sauvignon and Cliff House Red and White.

Coeur d'Alene Cellars (2002)
3890 N. Schreiber Way
Coeur d'Alene, ID 83814
208-664-2336
www.cdacellars.com

Coeur d'Alene Cellars was founded to create Rhone varietal wines from the Columbia, Walla Walla and Yakima valleys of Washington State. Owned by Kimber Gates, a graduate of Whitman College in Walla Walla with an MBA from Washington State University, and her parents, Dr. Charlie and Sarah Gates. The winemaker is Warren Schutz, graduate of UC, Davis with experience in both the California and New Zealand wine industries.

The winery produces over 3000 cases a year using grapes from several different AVAs including Walla Walla Valley, Red Mountain and Rattlesnake Hills. They produce single vineyard Syrahs, Chardonnay and a Mourvedre.

The winery operates Barrel Room No. 6, a tasting room/wine bar with light food and music at 503 East Sherman, Coeur d'Alene. Sarah is a landscaper, culinary expert and artist. She coordinates her talents at the tasting room and on the website. You can get artisan cheeses at the tasting room and recipes on their website.

The Merlot grape has roots going back to the first century in France. (Pun intended) The Merlot grape is often picked early in the harvest. It is common to pick Merlot up to three weeks before the Cabernet Sauvignon grapes in the same vineyard. The world's most famous producer is Chateau Petrus. A retail store in Missouri sold one 750 ml bottle of 1982 Petrus for $7799.00.

GRANDE RONDE CELLARS
Spokane, Washington.

Grande Ronde Cellars (1997)
906 W. Second Ave.
Spokane, WA 99201
509-455-8161
www.granderondecellars.com
Hours 12:00 pm to 6:00 pm (Wed-Sat)

Grande Ronde is a winery. Grande Ronde has its own rows of grapes. Grande Ronde has it own off-site tasting facility. Grande Ronde sells both retail and wholesale. We mention this because in Washington it is possible to have the best fruit even if you don't own the vineyard; to have a great facility, even if it is shared; to have a presence in the community with an off-site tasting room that supports local artists and to import foods that enhance the experience of wine drinking like olive and avocado oils, teas, barbecue sauces and other gourmet products.

Vineyard Control: working with the managers at Seven Hills and Pepper Bridge vineyards, Grande Ronde prunes its crop to yield a little over two tons per acre. The grapes are hand picked and processed at the winery location on Mount Spokane.

Grande Ronde ages their wine in 100% French oak barrels for 14 to18 months (40% new, 60 % one to two year old barrels) and then bottle ages the wine three to four years, releasing their wines when they are ready to drink. This philosophy has helped them garner 90+ scores from the *Wine Spectator*.

Their winery facility is in the foothills of Mount Spokane. John Mueller oversees the daily operations at the winery and Dave Westfall does the marketing and off-site tasting room. Dave was a wine retailer and caterer from 1980 to 1986 and then started a wholesale distributorship business from 1986 to 2000. (OK, so I'm also writing this book.) John's brother, Dr. Michael Manz (1948 - 2006) was one of the partners and original winemaker. The fourth partner, David Page, is a world renowned wine collector who also had ties to the wholesale wine business.

Latah Creek Wine Cellars (1982)
13030 East Indiana
Spokane, WA 99216
509-926-0614
www.latahcreek.com
Hours: 9:00 am to 5:00 pm (Daily)

Mike Conway came to the northwest in 1980 to work at Worden Winery after a California wine career that saw him begin at E and J Gallo winery in 1972 as a micro biologist and then take a similar position at Franzia Brothers in 1975. In 1977 he became an assistant winemaker at Parducci before coming to Washington to work in 1980 at Worden's winery.

In 1982 two new wineries were opened that Mike worked at simultaneously – Hogue Cellars and his own startup winery, Latah Creek. Two years later Mike went his own way and focused on Latah Creek. Mike's wife, Ellena, oversees the business aspects of the business as well as the tasting room and gift shop. Their daughter, Natalie, joined the business in 2005 as an assistant winemaker.

Floyd Broadbent, Yakima artist, creates the label for Latah Creek. The labels often depict flocks of birds rising from the marshes including pheasant, wood duck and Canada geese.

The tasting room has a large selection of gift and food items in addition to their large selection of wines which includes Chardonnay, Huckleberry, Spokane Blush, Maywine, Moscato, Merlot and Sangiovese. The annual production at Latah Creek is 17,000 cases with 10% of that production dedicated to red wine.

> **The Cabernet Sauvignon grape** originated in the Bordeaux region of southwest France. Although the grape is relatively new (it is the result of breeding cabernet franc with the sauvignon blanc grape in the 17th century) it is so tolerant to different soils and climates that it is grown in almost all of the wine producing countries of the world including France, United States, Australia, Italy, Chile and South Africa. A 750 ml bottle of 1869 Mouton (Cabernet) sold for $13,000.00

Lone Canary (2003)
109 South Scott St.
#B2
Spokane, WA 99202
509-534-9062
www.lonecanary.com
Hours: 12:00 pm to 5:00 pm (Thurs-Sun)

Lone Canary Winery is owned by Steve Schaub, Mike Scott and Jeanne Schaub. After being raised on steak and kidney pie in England Mike Scott came to the United States and began his winemaking career at Worden's winery under the tutelage of Mike Conway. He then went to Steven Thomas Livingstone (which was purchased by Caterina). Mike Scott left Caterina and turned his attention to his own winery in 2003.

The winery's name comes from the Washington State Bird, the American Goldfinch, which is also known as the Wild Canary. After a large company with the name "Wild" in it brought a lawsuit over the word the owners changed the name to Lone Canary – which in the wine industry is now the unofficial code name for the Washington State bird. The staff refers to the logo bird as "Clooney."

Lone Canary has embraced the modern world and has developed a facebook site. They produce several Italian style red wines, Barbera, Sangiovese and an Italian blend, as well as a Sauvignon Blanc, Cabernet Sauvignon, Merlot and Birdhouse Red.

"Clooney"

Townshend Winery (1998)
16112 N. Greenbluff Rd.
Colbert, WA 99005
509-238-1400
www.townshendcellar.com
Hours: 12:00 pm to 6:00 pm (Fri-Sun)

Don Townshend is the owner/winemaker of Townshend Winery. While installing chilling units in Preston Winery in the early 1980s Don developed a desire to make his own wine. He experimented at home with fruit wines, Cabernet Sauvignon and Merlot. In 1998 he launched the winery and released his first wine in 2001.

His two sons, Michael and Brendon, are involved in the business. They have been learning the production side of the wine industry.

Don often ages his red wines from two to three years in both American and French oak. He produces more than twenty different wines and more than 10,000 cases of wine a year. His wines include Cabernet Sauvignon, Merlot, Syrah, Sweet Huckleberry Blush, Cabernet Port and a Chenin Blanc

Don has plans to open his winery in a newer, bigger facility in the Greenbluff area within the next couple of years.

Part II – The Geek Tour

Like Walla Walla one of the oldest wineries in the Spokane area is part of the Geek Tour. In Mountain Dome's case its founders Michael (1948-2006) and Patricia Manz had a unique vision to make sparkling wine in the tradition of France in Washington State. Their sparkling wines have been touted throughout the world by wine writers but their production is limited and they are open only on Saturdays during the summer so it is on the wine geek's tour.

Barili Cellars (2008)
608 W. Second Ave.
Spokane, WA 99201
509-995-4077
www.barilicellars.com

Russ Feist and Steve Trabun are owners/winemakers that started Barili Cellars. Their first releases will be in the spring of 2009. They include a 2008 Viognier from the Seth Ryan vineyards, a barrel fermented Chardonnay from Columbia Valley and a red blend of Cabernet Sauvignon and Syrah called Double Barrel Red (15% alcohol).

Barrister Winery (2001)
1213 W. Railroad Ave.
Spokane, WA 99203
509-465-3591
www.barristerwinery.com

Greg Lipsker and Michael White, attorney/winemakers, founded their winery in a garage. Barrister Winery has gone from the garage to a 100 year old building in the historic Davenport Arts District in downtown Spokane. (A building that once held an auto parts store. Perhaps they were supposed to be mechanics?)

In Spokane the growing season is too unpredictable and often too short to grow wine grapes, so, like many wineries in Washington State, Barrister sources its grapes from several different vineyards. Their Syrah is from Morrison Lane in Walla Walla. In addition they produce a Cabernet Sauvignon, Merlot, Cabernet Franc, Sauvignon Blanc and a red blend called Rough Justice.

Basalt Cellars (2004)
906 Port Dr.
Clarkston, WA 99403
509-758-6442
www.basaltcellars.com

The story begins in 2002 at the Grape Symposium when owners Rick Wasem, Don McQuary and Lynn DeVleming discovered one another and their shared passion for viticulture, winemaking and, they claim, wine drinking. The owners then immersed themselves in viticulture and enology classes at the Clarkston campus of Walla Walla Community College. The winery is named after the surrounding hills which are composed of basalt from past volcanic activity.

Bridge Press Cellars
16315 E. Temple Rd.
Spokane, WA 99217
509-991-3663

Brian and Melody Padrta's Bridge Press Cellars is the 600th winery in Washington State. Using the saignée method they plan to produce an intense Cabernet Sauvignon and a Merlot from the Walla Walla Valley appellation. Their first release will be the 2009 vintage.

Camas Prairie Winery (1983)
110 S. Main St.
Moscow, ID 83843
800-616-0214
www.camasprairiewinery.com

Stuart and Susan Scott started Camas Prairie in 1983 and lay claim to being Idaho's oldest independent winery. Camas Winery field crushes their grapes at their estate vineyard and then immediately presses the grapes at their winery. They produce a wide variety of wines including Lemberger, Gewurztraminer, Elderberry, Plum and TEJ Hopped Mead.

Caterina Winery (1993)
905 N. Washington
Spokane, WA 99201
509-328-5069
www.caterina.com

Opened in 1993 Caterina purchased the inventory of Stephen Thomas Livingstone. The winery is located near Riverfront Park (site of the 1974 World's Fair) in the historic Broadview Dairy Building. The winery has roots back to the 1880s where its ancestors, Luigi and Caterina Barbieri, had a winery in San Pietro Vara in Northern Italy. The tentacles of Caterina winemakers represented, at one time, more than 50% of the wineries in Spokane. The first winemaker at Caterina was Mike Scott who apprenticed under Mike Conway at Worden Winery in 1979. Worden is no longer with us. Mike Conway moved on to start Latah Creek Winery. Mike Scott put together a group of investors to purchase Steven Thomas Livingstone Winery and started Caterina Winery. After working at Livingstone and Caterina Mike Scott moved on to start Lone Canary. (At that time there were only eight wineries in Spokane including the now defunct Worden, Wyvern and Livingstone wineries.) Monica Meglasson, a native of Oregon, took over Scott's duties and is the current winemaker.

China Bend (1995)
3596 Northport-Flat Creek Rd.
Kettle Falls, WA 99141
509-732-6123
www.chinabend.com

Bart and Victory Alexander are the owners of this unique, maybe eccentric, winery vision. China Bend is an estate winery located on the banks of the Columbia River (Lake Roosevelt). Getting there is an adventure. You can take a seaplane or boat to access the winery via the Columbia River, or take a challenging road out of Kettle Falls to the property. The vineyard produces all of its own organic grapes that are used in the winery's organic, unsulfited wines. They also make some natural dessert wines as well as produce some wine from grapes they purchase in the Columbia Valley. Their list of wines includes Leon

Millot, Marechal Foch and several fruit wines. The property also has organic gardens where the owners grow fruits and vegetables for their organic gourmet foods.

Clearwater Canyon Cellars (2006)
1708 – 6th Ave N. Suite A
Lewiston, ID 83501
www.clearwatercanyoncellars.com

Patty Switzer is a co-owner and the winemaker at Clearwater Canyon Cellars. The winery is a vision of eight friends who wanted to bring the wine industry back to the Snake and Clearwater Rivers valley. The first grapes were brought into the Lewiston area by French born Louis Delsol in the 1870s. In 1883 Robert Schleicher acquired land on the south side of the Clearwater River about three miles east of Lewiston and planted a vineyard. By 1900 there were 80 acres planted in grapes. Another 180 acres were planted in 1887 by Jacob Schaefer. Over forty varieties of grapes were being grown and a 1908 Lewiston Tribune article said that the grapes had taken first prize over Californian wines in the last three great world's fairs. Prohibition came at the beginning of the 20th century and with it the demise of the vineyards. Clearwater Canyon Cellars is determined to revive the grape heritage. In 2006 they released a Malbec, a Carmenere and a red blend.

Colters Creek Winery (2008)
20154 Colter Creek Ln.
Julieatta, ID 93535
208-874-3933

Melissa Sanborn is the owner of this Idaho winery.

Emvy Cellars (2008)
16315 E. Temple Rd.
Spokane, WA 99217
www.emvycellars.com

Mark and Val Wilkerson (MV) are the owners of Emvy cellars. Their blend is called Devotion, a blend of 44% Merlot and 56% Cabernet Sauvignon from the Walla Walla Valley. The wine is aged in 100% French oak barrels, racked three times and coarsely filtered. The label was designed by Russian artist, Alexei Kazantsev. They have just gotten their off-site tasting room license at 906 West Second and join both Grande Ronde Cellars and Mountain Dome at the site.

Robert Karl (1999)
115 W. Pacific Ave.
Spokane, WA 99201
509-363-1353
www.robertkarl.com

Joe Gunselman and his wife, Rebecca, are the owners of Robert Karl winery. Joe uses his physician's knowledge of science and applies it to his wine making. A self-taught winemaker, he has continued his education by taking courses at University of California at Davis and the Walla Walla institute of Enology. Rebecca Gunselman oversees the marketing and winery operation. Robert Karl is a combination of family names. Robert comes from Rebecca's ancestry and Karl from Joe's. Robert Karl specializes in Cabernet Sauvignon, Syrah, Claret and Sauvignon Blanc. Their grapes come from the Horse Heaven Hills AVA.

Knipprath Cellars (1991)
5634 E. Commerce Ave.
Spokane, WA 99212
509-534-5121
www.knipprathcellars.com

Henning Knipprath first introduced his wines in 1991 and became a full time winery operation in 1999. The winery is located in the refurbished Parkwater School house. Henning's first career was as a military pilot. Knipprath produces several wines including Chardonnay, Merlot and a variety of ports and dessert wines including chocolate and vanilla ports. Henning Knipprath was born in Germany and grew up in Southern California.

Liberty Lake Wine Cellars (2005)
1028 S. Garry
Liberty Lake, WA 99019
509-255-9205
www.libertylakewinecellars.com

Doug and Shelly Smith are the owners and winemakers at Liberty Lake Cellars. They specialize in single vineyard wines from the Walla Walla Valley and Red Mountain AVAs. Liberty Lake is producing a Merlot, Cabernet Sauvignon and Syrah.

Life Force Winery (1989)
1193 Saddle Rd.
Moscow, ID 83843
208-882-9158

Life Force is listed in Dan McFeeley's "list of commercial meaderies." They produce huckleberry and raspberry honey wines as well as two different meads. The shop, Life Force Naturals, specializes in honey products. We encourage this to be on your unique shop radar sites.

Merry Cellars (2004)
245 Paradise St.
Pullman, WA 99163
509-338-4699
www.merrycellars.com

Winemaker Patrick Merry is from Montana. He released his first wines in 2004 including a Chardonnay, Cabernet Sauvignon, Syrah and Merlot. They source their fruit from Seven Hills Vineyard, Pepper Bridge, Stillwater Creek and Les Collines. The tasting room is located in the historic Old Post Office building. It is the first winery in Pullman, Washington, home to Washington State University, a leader in viticulture academia.

Mountain Dome Winery (1984)
16315 E. Temple Rd.
Spokane, WA 99217
509-928-2788
www.mountaindome.com

Mountain Dome began production of its sparkling wines in 1984. The flagship wine is a non-vintage brut with gnomes on the label. The gnome family bears a "sparkling" resemblance to the Michael and Patricia Manz family, owners of Mountain Dome Winery. Dr. Michael Manz (1948-2006) worked with his wife, Patricia, to make Mountain Dome a leader in the sparkling wine industry.

Mountain Dome has received numerous 90+ point ratings from reviewers around the world. In addition to their non-vintage they make a Vintage when the year is perfect, a Cuvee Forte (their reserve sparkling wine) and a Brut Rose.

Erik Manz took over the reigns of winemaker after his father, Michael, passed away. The winery is a family operation and all of the gnomes have worked in the winery. Michael's brother, John Mueller, has been cellar master since the first commercial production in 1988. The winery introduced a line of still wines under the label Pleasant Prairie. The wines include Chardonnay and Pinot Noir.

The sparkling wine is fermented in French oak barrels. Raphael Brisbois (Piper Sonoma, J in California) was their consultant in the beginning stages of the project. The winery was built by Michael, Patricia and Michael's brother, John. It is a state of the art, temperature controlled building in the foothills of Mount Spokane. The pressing is done near the geodesic dome (which was also built by the Manz family) and then gravity takes it underground to the stainless steel tanks in the main winery building. Hand crafted from the vineyards to the final product Mountain Dome has been another one of those visionary projects in Washington State wine history.

Nodland Cellars (2005)
E 11616 E. Montgomery
Suite #70
Spokane Valley, WA 99206
509-927-7770
www.nodlandcellars.com

Tim and Tracy Nodland began producing their Private Red Blend and Bebop Riesling in 2005. The red is a blend of Bordeaux varietals, and the Riesling is vinted dry. Tim is a jazz musician and promoter; Tracy is an oil painter. They began making wine together in their garage in 1999. Their appreciation of art is apparent in their label which was produced by Florida artist, Tim Rogerson. The label depicts a jazz band.

Overbluff Cellars (2007)
1427 Overbluff Rd.
Spokane, WA 99203
www.overbluffcellars.com

Overbluff is making three Cabernet Sauvignons – Latour Vineyard, Obsession and Triumph. A virtual winery at the moment.

Pend d'Oreille Winery (1995)
220 Cedar
Sandpoint, ID 83864
208-265-8545
www.powine.com

Owner/winemaker Stephen Meyer and his wife, Julie, started their wine career in Meursault, France working in the cellars after the 1985 harvest. They worked at several wineries and attended University of California at Davis during the late 1980s landing a position as Assistant winemaker at Roudon-Smith winery. They produce a Pinot Gris, Chardonnay, Viognier, Huckleberry Blush, Syrah and Merlot.

Pucci Winery
1055 Garfield Bay Rd.
Sandpoint, ID 83864

Timber Rock Winery (2005)
104 N. Fourth St.
Coeur d'Alene, ID 83814
208-777-9669
www.timberrockwine.com

Timber Rock is owned by winemaker/veterinarian Kevin Rogers and his wife, Michelle. Kevin is a guitar picking vet by day, works on his Cabernet at night. Michelle is an aero medical transport heath care professional by day and plans parties at night (presumably to get an audience for Kevin's guitar playing). Their dogs, Popeye and Pete, are head of security and the welcoming committee. Timber Rock produces Chardonnay, Merlot and Cabernet Sauvignon.

Vintage Hill Winery (2006)
319 Second Ave.
Spokane, WA 99201
509-624-3792
www.vintagehillcellars.com

Cody and Melissa George are owners of Vintage Hill with Brian and Heather Murray. Cody George is the winemaker. He uses French and Hungarian oak for aging. Vintage Hill produces a Syrah, Sauvignon Blanc and Merlot Rose.

Wawawai Canyon Winery (2005)
5602 State Route 270
Pullman, WA 99163
www.wawawaicanyon.com

The first commercial vineyard in Whitman County since prohibition, David and Stacia Moffett benefited from the help and encouragement of pioneering Lewiston viticulturist Bob Wing. A single test block was planted in 1994 with twelve different varietals. All of these were cuttings from Wing's vineyard. The vine survivor's finalists were Cabernet Sauvignon, Cabernet Franc, Lemberger, Sauvignon Blanc and Rkatsiteli. The have produced a Syrah and several blends. They will release their new red blend during the Lionel Hampton Jazz festival.

Watermark Cellar (2008)
North 10221 N. Comanche Drive
Spokane, WA 99208
509-467-8433

Watermark is a bonded Washington winery.

Whitestone Winery (2001)
115 NE Main St.
Wilbur, WA 99185
509-647-5325
www.whitestonewinery.com

Walter and Judy Haig started growing grapes in 1994 on their Grand Coulee Dam area property. They sold grapes to other wineries for several years until they started making their own wine in 2001. Their son, Michael, now takes care of the day to day operational and winemaker duties. They produce a Cabernet Sauvignon, Merlot and Cabernet Franc.

Part III

Day of the Dead Winery Tour

Sam and Dave Excursions

Cemetery

The young wine community has had some wineries close their doors for various reasons. We include them in our book so you will know some of the pioneers who are no longer with us and in some cases, never were.

Cannon Hill Vintners was the original proposed name of Vintage Hill. They fall into the category of never were.

Steven Thomas Livingstone began its life as a winery in 1989. The story goes that they were requested to change their name because it was too close to a winery's label in California and after careful consideration about whether to challenge the potential lawsuit the winery decided to close its door in 1992. (You might recall that other wineries in the state have had a similar problem which is why we have Covey Run instead of Quail Run and we haven't even begun yet in the Spokane cemetery.)

Wild Canary was the original proposed name of Lone Canary. An alcoholic company that had Wild in its name threatened to challenge the name of their new venture so they changed their name. They fall into the category of never were.

Worden Winery was the first winery to open in Spokane in 1980. Jack Worden released a lot of value oriented wines and had an extensive private label program. Worden was one of the first wineries to make a 50/50 Merlot-Cabernet blend, a trend that started with the Meritage movement in California. Worden's winery was one of the pioneers of the blended wine industry in Washington.

Wyvern Cellars was located in the old Worden winery Wyvern's fate was not much better than Worden's. Wyvern was the largest private labeler in the Pacific Northwest with an acre of manicured grounds complete with flower beds and a koi pond.

The Chardonnay grape is a classic white grape grown throughout the world. It came to prominence as a white wine in Burgundy and as a component of champagne in France. Dr. Carole Meredith has done extensive DNA research on the Chardonnay grape and concluded that it is a member of the Pinot family. She says that the grape is a cross between the Pinot and a nearly extinct grape called Gouais Blanc. The earliest reference to Chardonnay wine was written by Cistercian monks in 1330. You can buy a 750 ml bottle of 1985 Domaine Romanee Conti Montrachet (most renowned Chardonnay in the world) for $7700.

Part IV

GOTTA EAT—Spokane Area

Sam and I have been exploring the Spokane, Coeur d'Alene, Sandpoint and Pullman areas for food for more than a combined sixty years. The approach to these areas is a little different than Walla Walla.

People who come to Spokane often have other agendas than just winery hopping. If you can get a ticket you might be going to a Gonzaga University basketball game; you might be participating in one of the sporting events (Bloomsday or Hoopfest – you might see Sam and I at the coffee shop when you run by) or attending a Broadway play, or listening to a concert at the Opera House.

We have more than twenty wineries in the Spokane and Northern Idaho area which ranges north seventy miles to China Bend on the Columbia River to thirty miles west to Whitestone in Wilbur (not so good for eating options) to seventy miles northeast to visit Sandpoint or a hundred and ten miles south to visit the Pullman and Lewiston area.

During your visit you may want to take in a round of golf one day and a day of antique hunting on another. While you are exploring the wineries some of your group may want to visit our museums, universities or gardens. Most of the visitors will stay in the Spokane/Coeur d'Alene area where the majority of wineries are currently located. Here is how we would approach our food explorations.

Got an early tee time?

Dolly's Corner Café
1825 N. Washington
Spokane, WA 99205
509-325-9034

Dolly's Corner Cafe on North Washington near Ryne Sandberg field (North Central High School – one of the authors graduated from North Central as did Baseball Hall of Famer, Ryne

Sandberg) serves up some of the best breakfast in town and if you aren't interested in eggs and bacon you might check to see if they have any of their homemade cinnamon buns or pie available. Expect drip coffee here.

Fergusons Café
804 W. Garland Ave.
Spokane, WA 99205
509-325-3482

Located in the historic Garland District since 1935 (one of the authors graduated from nearby Shadle Park High School where real men wear kilts). Fergusons was used in the filming of both Vision Quest and Benny and Joon (remember Johnny Depp's dancing dinner rolls?) Try an omelet or scramble made with local Sonnenberg's sausage.

Frank's Diner (Breakfast)
1516 W. 2nd Ave.
Spokane, WA 99201
509-747-8798

Frank's is in an old railroad car (built as an observation car for the president of the Northern Pacific Railroad in 1906). The landscape is full of plateaus of chicken fried steaks, reservoirs of gravy and mountains of hash browns. Your eggs, bacon and sausages will be transferred from the hot grill to platters as you drink your coffee (this is the place to look for the guy on the donkey who sells mountain grown coffee, not to look for the staff member who competed in the regional barista contest) and drink out of non-breakable water glasses. (Remember how rough and tumble eating on a train can be.)

Spokane is a city of 197,000 residents with a metro area population exceeding 400,000 people. Rising 2000 feet above sea level it is the largest city between Seattle and Minneapolis. It was founded in 1872 and the original spelling was "Spokan" which means "Children of the Sun."

Knight's Diner (the original train car)
2909 N. Market St.
Spokane, WA
509-484-0015

Standard Gauge cooking here. Your hash browns are piled up in four-feet, eight and a half inch volcanic-like mounds where the smell of onions and gravy emanates like flowing lava. The Knight's Diner was the first breakfast train car in town. The railroad car (car No. 988 for you train historians) was built in 1906. During World War Two it was used as a classroom to support the war effort. In 1949 Jack Knight purchased the Pullman car, moved it to the corner of Division and Jackson streets and converted it into a dining car. When the General Store expanded in the 1990s the diner was moved from its Division Street location to the Hillyard location. The owners peel 100 pounds of potatoes every day and cool them over night. No frozen spuds here. Corned beef hash, eggs the way you want them (unless you want them poached or shirred, thems fighting words here).

Old European (European)
7640 N. Division St.
Spokane, WA 99212
509-467-5987

You can get Danish Aebelskivers, Dutch Babies, Swedish Crepes, Hungarian Goulash, Basil Soup, German Reuben on Dark Rye or German Potato Pancakes, if the French toast or four different types of eggs benedict don't tempt you; biscuits and gravy, omelettes, eggs and your choice of meat plus home made cinnamon rolls. If you want to make breakfast your meal for the day before your group goes its separate ways, or if you have six people who never seem to agree on a type of cuisine, then this is a good choice.

The Syrah grape is one of the oldest grape varietals in the Cotes du Rhone region of southern France. One legend says it arrived in France via the Phocaeans of Asia Minor who brought it from Shiraz, Persia. Most likely it is a combination of the Dureza and Mondeuse grapes and was well established in France by the 13th century.

Rocket Bakery
3315 N. Argonne Rd.
Spokane, WA 99212
509-927-2340

The Rocket Bakery's main establishment is in the Spokane Valley on Argonne Road but you will find their satellite bakeries throughout town. The Rocket has been pulling lattes for its customers and baking pastries since 1992. They are a throwback to the old style scone and muffin, lots of grains and fruits in those pastries.

Rockwood Bakery
315 E. 18th Ave.
Spokane, WA 99203
509-747-8691

The Rockwood Bakery is a gem. It is located on the south side of town near Manito Park. (Manito is a nice place to take a stroll or have a picnic and if you want an artist to make your coffee this is the place to go). The park has some spectacular gardens including a rose garden, a formal European style garden (Duncan Gardens), a Japanese garden and a year round conservatory (Gaiser Conservatory). Originally called Montrose Park its name was changed in 1903 to Manito which means "spirit of nature" in the local Indian language. Rockwood Bakery has my favorite latte in the area plus quiches, apple and cherry pies, home made granola, muffins and pastries. You can get an assortment of cookies for your journey to the wineries as well.

Skyway Café
Felts Field
Spokane, WA 99201
509-534-5986

Want to watch planes and helicopters taking off while you enjoy the best biscuits and gravy in Spokane? You can get a platter of breakfast that includes eggs, four strips of bacon, hashbrowns and toast.

Starbuck's, Jacob Java and a lot of nice places to drink coffee

We have several local and national coffee chains. Jacob Java (Washington and Sixth) is a good choice for a drive through latte. One of the first in Spokane they have a loyal clientele (that's where I start most of my road trips). You will find several Starbucks both as stand alone stores and in the usual suspect chain stores like Barnes and Noble at the Northtown Mall. There are a lot of other coffee shops and since you are in Washington most of them are going to be good or they would not have survived.

Want to do Lunch or Meet for dinner?

98Twenty (Bistro)
9820 N. Nevada
Spokane, WA 99208
509-468-9820

Ninety-eight twenty is a good place to go for small plates. The appetizers include bacon wrapped shrimp, lobster lollypops, truffle fries, asparagus tempura and a Greek antipasto. The bar is a comfortable place to sit and one of the few places with gourmet dining and big screen televisions. The dining area has a lot of room so you aren't sitting on top of another table. The entrees range from lobster risotto to a baseball cut steak to a red curry vegetarian dish. They have flights of wine in their tasting menu as well as a good selection of imported and local wines.

Ambrosia (Bistro)
9211 E. Montgomery
Spokane Valley, WA 99206
509-928-3222

Scott and Kay Cook are the owners of Ambrosia (and Café Neo on the north side). The lunch has small plates like pecan crusted brie, pan seared ahi, Szechuan green beans and a variety of soups and salads. The Cajun pasta has chicken and andouille sausage, shrimp, red bell peppers, red onions and mushrooms. I like this with a crisp Sauvignon Blanc or a bolder Chardonnay (goes nicely with the cream sauce). In the evening you can get larger portions of the above or try their chicken picatta, rack of lamb, gnudi (ricotta dumplings), rib eye steak, crab ravioli or butternut squash ravioli.

Anthony's (Seafood)
510 N. Lincoln St.
Spokane, WA 99201
509-328-9009

You might see a few fish jumping at Anthony's, a chain from Seattle that serves fresh seafood. This spot has always boasted one of the premier views of the Spokane Falls. Anthony's signature dishes include coconut prawns, Dungeness crab cakes and alder planked salmon. The meals start with a salad or cup of clam chowder. You can get other things here but I would concentrate on the seafood and the view.

Aqua (Small plates)
30 W. Sprague Ave.
Spokane, WA 99201
509-747-2111

Aqua is a small plates restaurant that has a lot of energy flowing in it on Friday and Saturday evenings. You could get the habanero cilantro lime scallops satay or the ginger orange braised short ribs or order from the sushi menu. We usually get the duck roll.

Azar's (Greek)
2501 N. Monroe St.
Spokane, WA 99205
509-326-7171

If you want Mediterranean food Katy at Azar's has been serving up Greek food for more than twenty years. She has a buffet during the week which is one of the best bargains in the city. Greek salad, lentil soup, gyros, hummus, feta cheese, falafel and chicken kabsa. We are talking Formica top tables, an outside hookah bar and belly dancing on Friday evenings. If you want a thick, Greek coffee you can have one while you are smoking tobacco from one of their large, ornate water pipes. The tobacco is shisha or a sticky, confectionary mixture of tobacco, molasses and fruit. (You can even choose your flavor of fruit from double apple to pineapple).

Bangkok Thai
1325 S. Grand
Spokane, WA 99202
509-838-8424

The owners decorated the restaurant with sculptures and sandstone statuary that was shipped directly from Thailand. They have the traditional appetizers of chicken satay, spring rolls as well as fried tofu, crab in the blanket and fried calamari. The hot and sour chicken soup (Tom Yum Kai) is one of my favorites with mushrooms, lime juice, lemon grass, chili paste, cilantro and lime leaves. They have a large assortment of salads from Laab Kai (chopped chicken, red onion, Thai chili, lime juice and mint leaves to my favorite Yum Neau (savory beef salad) with beef, cucumber, red onion, tomato, mint leaves and cilantro with dressing. They have a large selection of curries from green curry in coconut milk to a red curry with prawn and pineapple. They have one of the best selections of noodle and vegetarian dishes in town. This is a good place for a large group and they are open on Sunday afternoons so if you do some wine tasting during the day you have a spot to gather in the late afternoon for dinner. Bangkok Thai has opened a second location at 1003 East Trent.

Bennidito's (Pizza)
1426 S. Lincoln
Spokane, WA 99204
509-455-7411

Bennidito's has margarita pizza (olive oil based, mozzarella, Romano cheese, fresh tomatoes and basil) or wrap yourself around their meat primo (mozzarella cheese, pepperoni, salami, Italian Sausage, prosciutto ham, pancetta bacon, meatball & Canadian bacon). The Greek Primo has mozzarella and feta cheese, kalamata and green olives, roasted red peppers and pepperocini. Calzones? Of course you can get a marinated chicken or meat calzone but even Edesia, Roman goddess of food, would like their Greek calzone filled with green olives, feta cheese, roasted red peppers, pepperocini and kalamata olives or their New Yorker with ricotta, fresh mushrooms, artichoke hearts and olive oil garlic sauce. (Note: Like us the gods have been known to cross cultural lines if the pizza pan is tempered with extra virgin olive oil.)

Café Marron (Bistro Mediterranean)
144 S. Cannon St.
Spokane, WA 99201
509-456-8660

Café Marron is owned by the people from Luna, William and Marcia Bond. The neighborhood restaurant in Browne's Addition specializes in food and wines from the Pyrenees. The breakfast menu is quiche Lorraine, duck eggs chorizo, corned beef hash, baked ham and eggs and a daily omelet. The entrees include a café Reuben, rigatoni, saffron mussels, cilantro lime tuna, vegetable curry, seared halibut and pan roasted chicken breast. This is a comfortable dining room, tucked away on the west side of town a few block from the museums.

Café Neo's (Bistro)
10208 N. Division St.
Spokane, WA 99218
509-467-5961

The same people who bring you Ambrosia. Pecan crusted Brie, sausage and lentil soup, grilled portabella sandwich, crab cake po' boy, porcini scallops and spicy prawn pasta. See Ambrosia

Catered for You (Anything, just ask Romeo)
732 N. Crestline St.
Spokane, WA 99202
509-624-9686

Looking for gourmet catering? Call Chef Romeo Herrera at Catered for You. I've cooked with Romeo on several occasions as well as attended events he has catered. Try one of his specialties from his native Latin American roots or pork tenderloin with red pepper sauce. He also teaches cooking classes at his catering location.

Chicken-N-More
414 ½ W. Sprague Ave.
Spokane, WA 99201
509-838-5071

This is your hole in the wall place for Southern fried chicken, barbecue ribs, pulled pork sandwiches, collard greens and baked beans. Owner Bob Hemphill has his little screen television on any time there is a baseball game and if it isn't a squeeze bunt situation he will serve you up a cornmeal-breaded catfish dinner. The catfish is cooked to order so sit down and enjoy the game while you wait for your dinner to arrive, or if it isn't busy lean on the counter and marvel at how so little a space can put out so much Southern food.

Clinkerdagger (Continental)
621 W. Mallon Ave.
Spokane, WA 99204
509-328-5965

Clinkerdagger's, which is part of the Restaurants Unlimited group (Palamino, Cutter's, etc.), serves continental fare with a great view of the Spokane River. They serve up chicken, duck, pork and beef along with shellfish, salmon and fresh fish specialties. They also have a signature rock salt roasted prime rib; go early if you want it rare to medium-rare. This is another one of those throwback restaurants where you will recognize most of the items on the menu and your plate. Both the food and wine are priced for the view (steaks. crab legs and prime rib $33 to $40). However, if you want to go for a drink and sit in the pub area (where they have Charles Dickens plates on the wall) for Happy Hour from four to six or after nine in the evening, they have a large selection of reduced priced appetizers and bar drinks.

Davenport Hotel (Continental)
Palm Court & Peacock Lounge Restaurants
10 S. Post St.
Spokane, WA 99201
509-789-6848

The Davenport Hotel has one of the premier lobbies on the West Coast. It was opened in 1914. It was the first hotel with air conditioning. You could get a Crab Louis (named after Louis Davenport). The restaurant and Hall of Doges ballroom were considered two of the finest in the country. Their guests included Charles Lindbergh, Amelia Earhart, Mary Pickford, Clark Gable, John Philip Sousa, Bob Hope, Spokane's own Bing Crosby and Zane Grey and Dashiell Hammet wrote scenes based on the hotel. Almost every president in the twentieth century has stayed at the Davenport. There is a great collection of photographs displayed on the mezzanine.

The food at the Davenport is good hotel food but I wish it were the best in the West again. The dining room is tucked away in the corner of the hotel so you can't really see the magnificent lobby. (Go see the lobby - it is truly one of the best spots to sit and sip a beverage in the entire country. You have to give kudos to Walt and Karen Worthy for keeping this hotel out of the cemetery listing). The restaurant has steaks, halibut, salmon and chicken with a signature or Caesar salad. I actually prefer to go to the Peacock Lounge for lunch where you can absorb the history of the building and get a good Reuben sandwich or Scottish smoked king salmon vodka penne.

The Riesling grape is considered one of the noble grape varieties in the world and in 2008 surpassed the Chardonnay grape as the top white wine harvested in Washington State. Its origins are from the Rhine region of Germany. There are references dating back to the 15th century in both Germany and Alsace. The most expensive Rieslings are late harvest dessert wines. A 375 ml bottle of 1996 Kracher Trockenberenauslese Riesling sold for $800.00 bottle.

De Leon (Mexican Store & Deli)
102 E. Francis Ave.
Spokane, WA 99208
509-483-3033

De Leon (Mexican)
825 W. Riverside
Spokane, WA 99201
509-747-2085

If you want a burrito go to De Leon's. You get taco truck flavors and a table to sit at while you eat them. They have colas hecho en Mexico and fresh tortillas. Their main outlet on Francis is a deli/store that makes tortillas daily as well as tamales, chile verde and other Mexican specialties. It is fun to poke around the store with a large pizza pan and select items from their bakery cases. You can also get those hard to find ingredients for your home cooking like epazote, dried hominy, several different types of chili powders and, of course, organs. (We aren't talking pipe organs here.) Both places have a salsa bar with several sauces with varying degrees of hotness, pickled peppers, onions and chips.

Downriver Grill (Continental)
3315 W. Northwest Blvd.
Spokane, WA 99205
509-323-1600

The Downriver Grill has become a staple of northwest Spokane. It is a neighborhood restaurant that takes pride in serving quality food at a neighborhood price. They have a large selection of salads and sandwiches (including a Sonnenberg sausage sandwich, food critic and author David Rosengarten rated this the best Italian sausage in the country) to go with their pasta dishes like puttanesca or Tuscan chicken linguini. Their entrees include Pork Osso Buco, Wild Pacific Sockeye Salmon, roasted duck and paella.

Elk (Pub food from the Culinary Institute)
1931 W. Pacific Ave.
Spokane, WA 99204
509-363-1973

The Elk Pub is micro brew, wine by the glass and pub food orchestrated by graduates of the Culinary Institute of Art (San Francisco cooking school). They serve up a ground lamb sandwich, Thai angel hair pasta, gumbo and specials that might include a pumpkin soup or a beef Bourgogne. I think some of the best food in Spokane comes out of this neighborhood pub. They also have a large selection of draught micro brews and daily specials.

Europa Pizzeria (Italian)
125 S. Wall St.
Spokane, WA 99201
509-455-4051

Europa Pizzeria is inside an historic brick building called the Atrium that used to house the Magic Lantern Theater, a Mexican restaurant (Mission San Juan), a spice shop and book store. Europa has managed to stay in business at this location because they offer pasta, pizza, lasagna and salads in a family atmosphere and at family prices. The bar is a comfortable area with couches where you can sit and have a glass of wine (beverage of choice in this book).

Gordy's Sichuan Café
501 E. 30th Ave.
Spokane, WA 99203
509-747-1170

I believe the best Chinese restaurant in Spokane is Gordy's Sichuan. It may seem odd that I think a six foot six plus blonde guy and his wife, Jaime, are serving up the best Chinese food in town but this hideout is amazing. My favorites include Dan dan noodles, Black Date Chicken, Ants climbing on a tree, Chinese dumplings and Sichuan eggplant. Don't expect the sweet and sour here to look like "number A" at other Chinese restaurants. The vegetables are crisp; spicy means it has a kick to it and if you want a little more spice ask for it hotter or ask for some sambal. The garlic black bean beef or Mongolian beef are excellent. The smoked pork with noodles is my favorite dish and if they don't appear on the menu, or on the daily specials board, ask Gordy if he can make the dish for you. All he can do is say no. If he seems a little put out and wants to know who told you about them say "Sam." (On the other hand, Gordy and Jaime are both there to please their customers and if they have time will accommodate your wishes. They will talk to you about their culinary journey and if you have an hour or two to spare will give you a discourse on disc golf. They have competed in many regional and national championships.) Note: You get a bowl and chopsticks to eat with; forks are under the counter and they will give you one if you ask for it.

Herbal Essence Café (Continental)
115 N. Washington St.
Spokane, WA 99201
509-838-4600

The Herbal Essence is near Auntie's bookstore in downtown Spokane. Their specialties include herb crusted salmon, pesto stuffed swordfish, yellow fin yakisoba and huckleberry top sirloin.

Huckleberry's Natural Markets
Whole Foods Concept and Bistro
Spokane Wine Company Retail since 1984
926 S. Monroe St.
Spokane, WA 99204
509-624-1349

If you want organic food and the best selection of wines Huckleberry's should be on your list. They have a large selection of salads, entrees, sushi and sandwiches in the bistro (many organic and/or gluten free). They also have over 200 micro brews and the most diverse wine selection in town. Lou Anne Moxcey has been managing the wine department since the store opened. Prior to opening the wine department at Huckleberry's she was co-owner of Spokane Wine Company on Hamilton Street. Lou Anne has been one of the pioneers in the Washington wine industry. She opened the Spokane Wine Company in 1984 and has been instrumental in promoting all facets of the wine industry in Spokane. She was also one of the first people to do tastings with winemakers like Hubert Trimbach (Alsace) and Cosimo Taurino of Italy. Her philosophy has been that you learn most about Washington wines by comparing them to the great wines of the world. I think her philosophy helps us find out how the Washington wine industry is doing. (And we are doing pretty well in most cases.)

Hu Hot Mongolian Grill
11703 E. Sprague
Spokane, WA 99206
509-891-8711

What are we doing with a Mongolian grill in a wine book? First, my son David said I never put restaurants in that his friends like. Second, this is a great place to take a group. Everyone can choose their own food and eat at their own pace. I like the Hu Hot because they make their own specialty sauces as well as provide ingredients to make your own sauce like garlic, ginger, hot oils and soy.

Italian Kitchen (Italian)
113 N. Bernard St.
Spokane, WA 99201
509-363-1210

The Italian Kitchen has chicken Marsala, chicken piccata, Tuscan chicken; cioppino, scampi and blackened halibut; lasagna, gnocchi, linguini with prawns, seafood puttanesca and spaghetti carbonara. You can choose a pasta platter with your choice of pasta and six different types of sauces. The restaurant's bar was a famous meeting place during the 1974 World Expo when it was the St. Regis.

The Chenin Blanc grape is from the Loire Valley of France. It can be used to make sweet wines, dry white wines, dessert wines and brandy. The Chenin Blanc grape or Pineau d'Aunis (Anjou) dates back to the 9th century. A bottle of Moulin Touchais 1959 Anjou sold for $475.00/bottle. A fifty year old Chenin Blanc!!

Latah Bistro (Continental)
4241 S. Cheney-Spokane Rd.
Spokane, WA 99224
509-838-8338

Latah Bistro is owned by Dave and Heather DuPree. They ventured away from downtown to open their eclectic restaurant (near Qualchan golf course). They have a large selection of appetizers and salads including a chili-beef lime salad that I order on a regular basis. Their entrees include pork osso buco, Idaho rainbow trout, New York steak with foie gras butter, several different types of gourmet pizzas and you might want to get their bucket of love, a tiny bag of chili-chocolate cakes. They have a good wine list and it is half price on Mondays.

Lindeman's (Bistro)
1235 S. Grand Blvd.
Spokane, WA 99202
509-838-3000

The granddaddy of the espresso business, the old person on the block is Lindeman's. Way before there was a coffee fad in Spokane Merrilee Lindeman and her brother, David, were serving up fresh breakfast and lunch entrees along with the best coffee in Spokane. They used a local roaster, Four Seasons, for their coffee. Four Seasons is another pioneer in the Spokane area – roasting beans when critics said no one would pay a dollar for a cup of coffee just because it was called a latte. Recently the hours have changed at Lindeman's and it is no longer serving food in the morning. That's too bad because it was only a few blocks from my house and they have one of the best coffee and tea bars in the city. The restaurant has a large selection of salads, pasta dishes and sandwiches. It is a great place for a group to have a glass of wine or coffee while you sample a dessert. They have an outdoor seating area.

Luna (Continental)
5620 S. Perry St.
Spokane, WA 99223
509-448-2383

The owners, William Bond and his wife, Marcia, have created a restaurant with a modern interior, fresh food concepts and state of the art wine cellar. They support many of local food artisans in the Inland Northwest. The executive chef, Anna Vogel, worked with Tom Douglas in Seattle for nine years before taking over the reigns at Luna. The luncheon menu has a number of salads, appetizers and soups. You can get a sampler plate of salads which might include Tuna tartar with avocado, tomato, onion and wasabi vinaigrette or my favorite the Luna signature salad with candied walnuts, dried cranberries, gorgonzola and red onion.

One of the ways to pick out a good sandwich stop is the bread and Luna has their own bakery, Bouzies. This makes the Cubano Pork sandwich or grilled chicken with bacon and brie cheese that much better. They have Idaho trout on their luncheon menu as well as hoisin glazed tofu or maybe a meatloaf or seafood gumbo special.

The dinner menu includes five different apple wood oven pizza selections, salads and diverse entrées from spaghetti with braised short rib Bolognese sauce to pumpkin risotto to Rock Cornish game hen to organic kurobata pork loin or a New York strip loin steak. They have a big selection of Northwest wines as well as a diverse selection of wines from around the world.

La Madeleine Café (Bistro)
707 W. Main Ave.
Spokane, WA 99201
509-624-2253

This chain restaurant started in Dallas in 1982. The concept is simple food with a French flair. The lunch menu is based around soup and sandwiches. You can get a French Dip on a Parisian baguette or the Le Pot Pie which is a rotisserie chicken breast, potatoes, carrots and onion in a rich white wine cream sauce. I also like the Mediterranean pasta dish with Portobello mushrooms, garlic, artichoke hearts tomatoes and kalamata olives tossed in basil infused olive oil and bowtie pasta.

Maggie's South Hill Grill (Lunch and Catering)
2808 E. 29th Ave.
Spokane, WA 99223
509-536-4745

Maggie's is about catering and home style cooking. Some of your choices include flat iron steak, fish & chips, white cheddar pasta, a flank steak or, my favorite, fish tacos. They also have a gluten free menu for those who have dietary restrictions. The atmosphere is more lunch oriented or gourmet take out. Both are good options.

Max at the Mirabeau (Continental)
1100 N. Sullivan Rd.
Spokane, WA 99037
509-922-6252

Max is located in the Mirabeau Hotel in the Spokane Valley. It has a large selection of appetizers from edamame and smoked diver scallops to smoked salmon & ricotta won tons or Thai pork wings. This hotel restaurant has a good selection of fish entrees but I go for the meat. You can get hand cut steaks, pepper steaks, veal morel, rack of lamb, kurabota pork chops, huckleberry baby back pork ribs, pancetta stuffed chicken or their flat iron steak with hunter sauce. This is one of those hotel restaurants that is worth the drive to go to dinner.

Melting Pot
707 W. Main St.
Spokane, WA
509-926-8000

Dip your way into the Swiss culture by experiencing fondue in the twenty-first century. The price for a fondue feast at the Melting Pot runs from $82 to $96 per couple plus beverages. (The past participle of the French verb fonder – to melt – is fondu. See, Mrs. McCarthy I said I would remember that.) The different feasts start with cheese fondue, then a salad and your choice of entrees which run from Filet Mignon

Florentine to Lobster Tail to Porcini and Portobello Sacchetti and you finish with a milk chocolate fondue.

Milford's Fish House (Seafood)
719 N. Monroe St.
Spokane, WA 99201
509-326-7251

Milford's has been in Spokane since the 1974 World's Fair and has always been about seafood. You get wooden booths and nooks and crannies at Milford's. The dishes vary from Alaska true cod "Boston scrod style," to a seafood sauté Diane. One of the reliable places for a lobster or whole Dungeness crab. They have steak, rack of lamb and chicken on the menu but it is way on the bottom of the page. Don't let that scare you. I've had the rack of lamb with jasmine rice and mortar & pestle Malaysian tamarind & fresh mint sauce and would order it again. In the old days I know that the Bloody Mary's were excellent. An amazing scientific fact is that the celery sticks actually stood up a little straighter if you had the bartender put in a dab of extra hot horseradish sauce.

Mizuna (Continental, Vegetarian)
214 N. Howard St.
Spokane, WA 99201
509-747-2004

Mizuna started out life in 1996 as a vegetarian restaurant. The owners Sylvia Wilson and Tonia Buckmiller had a vision to make Mizuna one of the best restaurants in the city and it often garnered the top spot from local food writers. After five years they added seafood and organic hormone free meat dishes to their menu but even to this day they have separate cooking surfaces for meats and vegetables. The original owners have handed down the reins to Michael Jones who has been a long time employee of Mizuna.

The grilled rack of lamb with kalamata olive vinaigrette and caramelized onion-parmesan Reggiano bread pudding is excellent as well as the pan seared Berkshire pork chops with polenta grits, queso fresco, sofrito and collard greens. But mostly I go to Mizuna because these people do know how to make vegetables taste like you are sitting at the king's table. I like the roasted beet and lentil salad with chevre cheese and candied walnuts. Flash fried tofu with jalapeno marinated cabbage, ginger cilantro aioli and spicy pecans as an appetizer or artisan cheeses, honey and salt & pepper almonds with figs, tree fruit and house-made fennel crackers. The vegetarian entrees range from potato gnocchi with crushed roma herb sauce to a grilled field roast with mushroom duxelles, blue cheese mashed Yukon gold potatoes, herbed broth and seasonal vegetables.

Moxie (Continental)
816 W. Sprague Ave.
Spokane, WA 99201
509-456-3594

Ian Wingate is the chef/owner of Moxie. He is one of the most decorated chefs in the county. He worked at Lark Creek Inn (with James Beard chef of the year, Bradley Ogden). After the California Culinary experience he was recruited to work at Roy's in Hawaii.

Ian does a lot of fusion cooking with a French flair. Soups? His daily special might be a lobster and butter nut squash soup; Ian always has a French onion gratinee and a miso soup on the menu. His appetizers usually include a grilled kai-Bi beef or black pepper and sea salt cured tuna. (AND if he has the white truffle and lobster mac-n-cheese au gratin get it. It won't remind you of home, but you will wish your mom had made it this way). He always has a selection of wok plates that include vegetarian, small planet tofu, hot and sour prawns or a filet mignon & prawns dish. Ian's pepper crusted breast of duck with a sweet Thai chili vinaigrette served over wok seared chow mein noodles with baby bok choy, shiitake mushrooms, bean sprouts, and broccolini in a sesame ginger sauce is killer. You can get a northwest paella or a tuna katsu (yellow fin tuna breaded in panko, seared rare with ginger lime butter sauce, sesame aioli and coconut jasmine rice) or do what I usually do for lunch, read the menu and then order Ian's signature dish, charbroiled chipotle glazed meatloaf.

Mustard Seed (Asian)
4750 N. Division St. (Northtown Mall)
Spokane, WA 99207
509-483-1500

    The Mustard seed began in 1978 in Missoula, Montana and moved to Spokane in the 1980s. Yes, we are including a restaurant that had its roots in Montana. They opened two restaurants in Spokane. One downtown on Spokane Falls Boulevard and the other on Sprague Avenue in the Spokane Valley. The one downtown moved to Northtown and the one in the Spokane Valley closed to make room for Winco Foods. (You probably won't get shrimp Osaka at Winco's deli).

    The lunches feature entrees like General Mustard's chicken, chicken Osaka, sweet and sour pork, beef teriyaki in a bowl with rice and Asian slaw or wok-fried bowls of hot & spicy pork and peppers, wok-fried vegetables, mushroom beef or halibut Osaka. My favorite dinner entrees are the bong bong chicken (stir fried vegetables, chicken in a wine sauce), Asian glazed pork ribs (oven roasted and glazed with hoisin sauce) and kung pao chicken noodle. Expansion has come in the form of the Noodle Express which now has three locations in Spokane and Coeur d'Alene.

Niko's (Greek)
725 W. Riverside Ave.
Spokane, WA 99201
509-624-7444

    Laith Elaimny, owner/chef, opened Niko's doors in 1985. His mother and father operated a restaurant on Dishman-Mica road for many years and many of his mother's recipes are in Niko's cookbook. Niko's appetizer menu includes a trio of hummus dips. The entrées vary from souvlakia shish kabob to moussaka layered casserole with eggplant, potatoes, beef and lamb in tomato and béchamel sauces topped with kasseri cheese. Chicken dishes include chicken breast kabsa with Laith's special 23 spice blend. Niko's is an upscale Greek restaurant. They usually have several different flights of wine that feature wines from around the world. The prices reflect the table cloth ambiance and large wine cellar.

O'Doherty's Irish Grille (Irish Pub)
525 W Spokane Falls Blvd.
Spokane, WA 99201
509-747-0322

O'Doherty's is a lot more about being in an Irish pub than it is about being a food establishment. You can get Patty's Scottish eggs, shepherd's pie, corned beef and cabbage and bangers & mash. Late at night they will still serve you a bowl of Irish beef and sausage stew, a Hooligan & Hannigan sandwich or fish & chips. You might want to be here, or not, depending on your partying style, for St. Patrick's Day. They drink Irish wine all day long (think Guinness) and all of the patrons claim some sort of Irish blood.

Onion (Gourmet Hamburger)
302 W. Riverside Ave.
Spokane, WA 99201
509-747-3852

The Onion has been serving up twelve different types of gourmet burgers from state of the onion to the jalapeno bacon since the 1980s.

Opa (Pizza)
10411 N. Newport Hwy.
Spokane, WA 99218
509-464-1442

Opa is both a pizzeria and a Greek restaurant. North side diners have finally got a neighborhood place to get flaming saganaki, spanakopita, pastitsio, souvlaki or a number of Italian dishes like lasagna, cannelloni or manicotti. They have fifteen different types of pizza, muffuletta sandwiches and open-faced foccacia bread sandwiches like mesquite chicken or "meat-a-ball." This is a good place to get Greek wine although there are different opinions as to what a good Retsina tastes like or if it is possible to get a good one.

Raw (Sushi)
723 W. First Ave.
Spokane, WA 99201
509-747-0556

Raw is another in the long list of sushi restaurants that have opened in Spokane over the past few years. My experience has taught me to go on Tuesday or Wednesday, the weekends are crowded and as the internet reviews attest, inconsistent. (In Spokane I don't eat much sushi on Mondays. I don't know if the fish really doesn't get delivered until Tuesdays here in the "inland" empire but my father's warning sticks in my mind every time I go out to dinner on a Monday night.)

Rock City Grill (Italian & American)
808 W. Main
River Park Square Mall
Spokane, WA 99201
509-455-4400

This restaurant is located in River Park Square. The menu caters to large groups and families. Their sandwiches range from a Thai chicken panino to a Rock City club croissant to a southwest chicken wrap. The pastas include myzithra cheese to pepperoni & sausage lasagna to smoked salmon tortellini. I usually get the apple bourbon pork chops in an apple bourbon sauce with a sun-dried tomato oregano compound butter. They also have steaks, seafood fettuccini and a house made meatloaf stuffed with sun-dried tomatoes, green peppers, onions and pesto.

Santé Restaurant & Charcuterie
404 W. Main
Spokane, WA 99201
509-315-4613

Jeremy and Kate Hansen opened their restaurant adjacent to Auntie's book store. The food ranges from house cured meats to a tofu & Anjou pear with flax seed crust, rissole potatoes and sauce Montepulciano. They have a vegetarian menu that vegetarians would like (instead of just sticking on a few broccoli items and calling your restaurant vegetarian friendly). They have celery root puree with jalapeno, crispy parsnip, and honey ginger in a port reduction sauce. They have a black currant quinoa dish with a black balsamic reduction sauce. The dinner menu also includes Idaho wild sturgeon with a house-made bacon and lentil du puy, carrot Vichy with a garlic & sage jus. You can also get Bigelow Farms pork with an onion brulee.

This isn't a coffee house attached to an independent book store (although Auntie's is an independent book store and we need to support those) but a gourmet restaurant with an innovative chef who is going out on a limb to give us house-made, local foods.

Sawtooth Grill (Family)
808 W. Main Ave.
River Park Square Mall
Spokane, WA 99201
509-363-1100

The Sawtooth Grill caters to families who are shopping the downtown stores or going to movies in River Park Square. They have fourteen different burgers including four different Bison burgers. The Cobb salad cabin style is one of the best in town with a creamy balsamic dressing, smoked turkey, pepper bacon, tomato, hard-cooked egg, crumbled blue cheese, avocado and croutons. You can get fish & chips, cabin mac-n-cheese, Bison stroganoff, pasta primavera or a Bison stew.

Scratch (Continental)
1007 W. First Ave.
Spokane, WA 99201
509-456-5656

For people going to a concert or play downtown Scratch has a late night menu which includes Kobe Tri Tip steak (from snake river farms served with a pepper bacon veal au jus), Soba stir-fry (sweet and spicy with soy, soba noodles, vegetables and choice of duck, ahi, scallops, planet tofu or prawns), and Duck Breast (pan seared, apple, pancetta, pine nut risotto with orange maple glaze), Italian vegetable tian (eggplant, roasted red peppers, onions, elephant garlic, artichoke hearts, roasted tomatoes, asiago, mascarpone, ricotta, mozzarella, basil on a bed of boursin creamed spinach), rack of lamb with pomegranate molasses glaze), scratch hot pot (scallops, prawns, lobster, clams, mussels, andouille sausage, garlic, red peppers, onions, basil, fingerling potatoes and spicy tomato broth).

CI Shenanigan (Continental)
332 N. Spokane Falls Court
Spokane, WA 99201
509-455-6690

C I Shenanigan is behind the Doubletree Hotel. The food is in the vein of amber ale chicken sandwiches, Thai chicken salad, seafood linguine Alfredo and grilled ribeye. View of river and a lively bar crowd are good reasons this restaurant has been here twenty years.

Spencer's (Steak)
322 N. Spokane Falls Court
Spokane, WA 99201
509-744-2372

Spencer's is part of a chain that prides itself on aged, hand cut steaks. They start at $36.95 for the Spencer steak and go up to $48.95 for the Porterhouse steak. You can get lamb chops, pork chops, chicken, salmon, crab legs. Side dishes are extra. Is it expensive? I would say yes. Is it worth it? I like to go to Spencer's for a special evening out and they have always cooked the steaks the way everyone at the table wants their's cooked. A feat not accomplished everywhere you go. The wine list has been carefully chosen to complement the food; the dining room is inside the Doubletree hotel.

Stir
7115 N. Division
Spokane, WA 99208
509-466-5999

Stir is a North side neighborhood restaurant located in a strip mall on Division Street. The food is creative – spicy calamari appetizer, shellfish linguine, salmon with a beurre blanc, hangar steak. This place has a thoughtful wine list, good prices and lots of energy.

Sushi.com (Sushi)
430 W. Main
Spokane, WA 99201
509-838-0630

Sushi.com has a lot of loyal followers. The sushi is fresh and they have a number of Japanese dishes (even Teriyaki) that can satisfy those non-sushi eaters. Sometimes I just go there to have one of the noodle dishes and everyone stares at me through their fish eyes.

Taco Wagons (always on the move)

Washington Street – -- Between Sprague and First
and
North Division near Queen

Good spots to grab a taco while you are visiting one of the eight wineries in the downtown Spokane area.

Taste of India (Indian)
3110 N. Division St.
Spokane, WA 99207
509-327-7313

We have had several Indian restaurants come and go in Spokane -- the Taste of India has survived. The location is one reason. It is on the busiest street in the city. They have a good value luncheon buffet. The food isn't very hot but you can ask for some hot mango pickle or put some of the onion sambal on top of your food.

The Grand Vidure grape is also known as Carmenere. It originated in the Medoc region of Bordeaux, France. The name Vidure is a local Bordeaux name for a Cabernet Sauvignon clone. The phylloxera plague of 1867 destroyed nearly all of the Grand Vidure vineyards in Europe. The grape was rediscovered in Chile by Professor Boursiquot in 1994 and officially recognized as Carmenere in 1998.

Thai on 1st (Thai)
411 W. First Ave.
Spokane, WA 99201
509-455-4288

The godfather of Thai restaurants is Thai on First. Val trained many of the cooks who went out and started their own restaurants, who trained cooks … Soups, salads, stir fry, curry and noodle dishes.

Twigs (Continental)
808 W. Main Ave. (Downtown)
Spokane, WA 99201
509-232-3376

4320 S. Regal St (south hill)
509-443-8000

401 E Farwell (north side)
509-465-8794

Twigs is a martini bar with excellent, recognizable food. You can get steaks, kahlua pork, steak penne, seafood or a white truffle prosciutto pizza. Good to stop in before a movie, for an afternoon tapas lunch or dinner.

Two Seven Public House
2727 S. Mount Vernon
#5
Spokane, WA 99223
509-473-9766

The same people who bring you the Elk Pub in Spokane and the Moon Time in Coeur d'Alene. Culinary experienced pub chefs with a good selection of micro brews. See the Elk for more details.

Villaggio (Italian)
2013 E. 29th
Spokane, WA 99203
509-532-0327

Villagio has fresh organic basil, buffalo mozzarella and red sauce pizza (lactose-free) and a specialty pizza with figs, prosciutto di Parma, gorgonzola, olive oil, caramelized onions and balsamic-port reduction. Their insalata Villagio salad has organic mixed greens, fresh pears, caramelized onions and walnuts, gorgonzola with fig and balsamic vinaigrette.

Vin Rouge
3029 E. Twenty-ninth Ave.
Spokane, WA 99223
509-535-8800

Vin Rouge is both a gourmet restaurant and a place to meet friends for special menus and prices. On Monday they have 40% off wine (under $40/bottle). Their social hours (2:00 to 5:30 and 9:00 until closing) have a large selection of specialty drinks and micro brews at reduced prices along with salads and small plates that start at three dollars (vin rouge fries with aioli), to grilled chicken sandwiches and a vin rouge French dip panini or spiced lamb masala sandwich with spinach, myzithra cheese, kalamata olives with tzatziki on grilled pita.

Wild Sage (Continental)
916 W. 2nd Ave.
Spokane, WA 99201
509-456-7575

The Wild Sage is freshly eclectic, Chef Alexa is a graduate of Le Cordon Bleu in Portland and she combines her classic training and creative tendencies with the freshest ingredients. (And I haven't had popovers served with my meals since the days of Anthony's Pier 4 in Boston back in the late 1960s). Small plates include Yukon taquitos with a chile lime avocado sauce and pig wings, a favorite of the Grande Ronde crowd after a special event, crispy pork osso buco with a spicy oyster sauce. The roasted pear salad with living watercress, gorgonzola, candied walnuts and prosciutto di san daniele is a wonderful salad with legions of flavors crossing over the taste bud battlefield. The dinner entrees run from Veal Saltimbocca (veal cutlets, sage and prosciutto ham, angel hair pasta tossed with chardonnay butter) to breast of duckling (pan seared, heirloom squash risotto, spinach-bacon sauté with grain mustard gastrique to natural black angus New York steak or pork tenderloin marsala (kurabuta black Berkshire pork).

The menu changes with the availability of fresh ingredients. Each year they have a month where they promote Hawaiian seafood specialties. They have also started a late night menu to accommodate the theater/concert crowd downtown. And I did I mention to leave room for the Apple tartine for dessert with home made ice cream. Wild Sage specializes in exotic cocktails for those who are looking for a Pomegranate martini or fresh squeezed margarita.

**The Authors cooking
Sam on left, Dave on right**

Part V

The Cemetery

Aint Gonna Eat There No More

A lot of restaurants have come and gone in Spokane. We can't put all of them in this book but we hope the ones we do will make you remember some of the past risk takers who tried to enlighten us about both cuisine and wine.

Amore was Chef Gina Lanza's Italian eatery in Spokane. Hard to forget the bowling ball in the wall décor; her food was just as unique. Gina was Italian with a flare, the best puttanesca to come through Spokane and a pioneer in food and wine pairings in the area.

Ankeny's Rooftop at the Ridpath Hotel. Famous for its prime rib and view of the city.

Bombay Palace, Indian, One of Spokane's best ethnic restaurants couldn't make it at the West Second Avenue location – an address that has seen several restaurants come and go. Mark it "sad to say good-bye."

Chapter 11 – the venerable Prime Rib joint finally lived up to its name.

Churchill's Steak House – Burned down in 2008. A high end steak house that might rise from the ashes some day.

Fugazzi, International – its beginnings were a great bakery and international cuisine. A new restaurant will emerge in this location next to the Lusso Hotel.

Howard Street Café – Chef Sheila Collins was way ahead of her time with slow cooking and an array of fresh salads. She spawned Catered for You.

The Ivy—We would be remiss if we were exclude this high end Continental restaurant from the cemetery as it was located in a former funeral parlor.

Laskar's was one of a long line of restaurants in the Lincoln Heights shopping center location. They served Caribbean and Mediterranean cuisine. Prior to Laskar's there were several other restaurants including Café **Roma**, a Middle Eastern restaurant.

The Mars Hotel – This fine restaurant (Il Moon Café) was headed by talented chef Steve Quinones (La Leyenda). The hotel went bankrupt and mysteriously burned to the ground.

Moreland's – Chef Billie Moreland's eatery, she was ahead of her time with fresh, local ingredients.

Oliveto's was the best Italian restaurant we have had in Spokane. Provimi Veal, aged beef, home made pasta and sauces. Dori and Arnie Klein left some sad customers when they moved to California and Dori took her hand dipped chocolate recipe with her.

Paprika was one of the best restaurants to come through Spokane with Chef Karla Graves at the burners. After a decade she and her husband decided to close down the eclectic restaurant on South Grand Boulevard.

Patsy Clark's Mansion was one of the first of the high end gourmet eateries with an extensive wine list. It was located in a lavish turn of the century mansion. (Think Tiffany window, Italian artisan carved beams, angels floating in ceiling paintings.) It was said that the wine cellar was haunted.

St. Regis Café – this cozy, intimate spot was known for exceptional Northern Italian cuisine and a wine list to match.

Spokane House had customers coming from Seattle and Portland for the stunning view of the city, outstanding cuisine and perhaps the best wine cellar in the state. The first Mouton I ever drank was here.

Part VI

GOTTA SLEEP (Spokane)

Cavanaugh's River Inn
700 N. Division St.
Spokane, WA 99202
509-326-5577

Davenport Hotel & Tower
10 S. Post St.
Spokane, WA 99201
509-455-8888

Doubletree
322 N. Spokane Falls Court
Spokane, WA 99201
509-455-9600

Fotheringham House B&B
2128 W. Second Ave.
Spokane, WA 99201
509-838-1891

Hampton Inn
2010 S. Assembly St.
Spokane, WA 99224
509-747-1100

Hilton Garden Inn
9015 W. Hwy. 2
Spokane, WA 99224
509-244-5866

Holiday Inn Express
801 N. Division St.
Spokane, WA 99202
509-328-8505

Hotel Lusso
1 N. Post St.
Spokane, WA 99201
509-747-9750

Mirabeau Park Hotel
1100 N. Sullivan Rd.
Spokane Valley, WA 99037
509-924-9000

Montvale Hotel
1005 W. First Ave.
Spokane, WA 99201
509-747-1919

Ramada Inn
8909 Airport Rd.
Spokane, WA 99201
509-838-5211

West Coast Hotel
303 W. North River Dr.
Spokane, WA 99202
509-838-2711

"It is an art apart, Saint Francis of Assisi said, "All saints can do miracles, but few of them can keep hotel." Twain, *Notebook*

"The only way to keep your health is to eat what you don't want, drink what you don't like, and do what you'd rather not." Mark Twain, *Following the Equator*

Part VII

GOTTA EAT Coeur d'Alene

Although Coeur d'Alene does not offer an abundance of wineries to visit both Coeur d'Alene Cellars and Timber Rock have downtown tasting rooms. It is convenient to coordinate a little wine tasting with a walking tour of the town's many fine art galleries, a round of golf, a day on the lake or dinner.

Angelo's (Italian)
846 N. Fourth St.
Coeur d'Alene, ID 83814
208-765-2850

Angelo's Ristorante has become a favorite of locals seeking a quiet, romantic evening out. Chef Angelo and wife Julie reside over the cozy dining room serving up traditional Italian fare made with organic ingredients. Veal Menu – saltimbocca, parmigiano, scallopini or Marsala or Chicken Menu—sotto cielo, milano, mediteranneo or Parmigano.

The Beachhouse (Continental/Casual with lake view)
3204 Coeur d'Alene Lake
Coeur d'Alene, ID 83816
208-664-6464

Here's a place you can pull your car into the parking lot, or your boat into the dock, to dine on steaks, seafood and enjoy spectacular sunsets.

The Semillon grape is a prolific grape and at one time was considered to be the most planted grape in the world. In the early 1820's the grape covered 90% of the vineyards in South Africa. The classic Bordeaux white wine is a blend of Semillon and Sauvignon Blanc. As a sweet wine Chateau d'Yquem uses about 80% Semillon in their sauternes blend. (A "recent" bottle of 1893 Chateau d'Yquem sold for $13,787.00.)

Beverly's (Fine dining with a view)
Coeur d'Alene Resort Hotel
Wine Spectator Award Winner
115 S. Second St.
Coeur d'Alene, ID 83814
208-765-4000

For a special evening out with gourmet food, fine wine and a stunning view, Beverly's, located on the seventh floor of the Coeur d'Alene Resort, is our top choice. Typical appetizers include a Charcuterie platter with house made prosciutto or bison carpaccio. Entrées feature prime graded beef or the likes of seared Muscovy duck breasts with goose confit and spiced rubbed foie gras. We consider the extensive wine list to be one of the best in the Northwest. (Sam was the wine steward there for 18 years Note: you couldn't find him in the back room there either.)

Bistro on Spruce (Bistro)
1710 N. Fourth St.
Coeur d'Alene, ID 83814
208-664-1774

Tapas menu is served from 3:00 to 5:30. Features include Ahi tuna, Moroccan meatball with feta cream sauce and classic Caesar.

Café Carambola (Latin American – lunch only)
610 W. Hubbard
Coeur d'Alene, ID 83814

If you are in the mood for a quick bite on the run consider Café Carambola, a tiny spot in Harbor View Plaza on NW Boulevard on the way into town. The charming husband and wife team (she is the chef, he runs the front) offer delicious Latin-American fare with vibrant, fresh flavors. Don't let the storefront fool you, this is a place with outstanding, flavorful food.

Capones Sports Pub (More taps than tables)
751 N. Fourth St.
Coeur d'Alene, ID 83814
208-667-4843

Capone's is a popular Pub with a huge selection of beer on tap, good pizza and big, messy hoagie-style sandwiches.

The Cedars Floating Restaurant
(Continental /Casual with lake view)
1 Marina Dr. Blackwell Avenue
Coeur d'Alene, ID 83814
208-664-2922

The Cedars Floating Restaurant has been a Coeur d'Alene landmark since 1965. Recently renovated, and with Chef Miles in the kitchen, the food quality, service and ambiance match the view. On a warm evening, this is a good place to enjoy an appetizer and a glass of wine or a cocktail on the deck.

Fleur de Sel (French)
(Same building as Highlands Day Spa)
4365 E. Inverness Dr.
Post Falls, ID 83854
208-777-7600

This new addition to the restaurant scene features regional French Bistro and Northern Italian cooking. Owners Laurent and Patricia met in Nice, France and have worked in the hospitality industry from Cannes to Billings, Montana to San Francisco to Post Falls Idaho. The charming and attentive Patricia resides over the small dining room which has an intimate, relaxed feel. I have enjoyed scallops and prawns in a vermouth sauce, the duck sausage with duck leg confit and a classic steak poivre with bistro fries.

Hudson's Hamburgers (just hamburgers – an institution)
207 E. Sherman Ave.
Coeur d'Alene, ID 83814
208-664-5444

Downtown is the venerable Hudson's. They have been making hamburgers since 1907. Counter-only, filled with locals enjoying small-town gossip, and old-fashioned hand formed hamburgers served with or without cheese. Pickles or onions, yes; lettuce, tomatoes, fries, shakes, NO. Don't even ask! But you can get their signature spicy ketchup.

Mexican Food Factory (Mexican)
1032 N. Fourth St.
Coeur d'Alene, ID 83814
208-664-0079

Fourteen different burritos, selection of tacos, tamales, burritos and a fillet of cod fish taco with cabbage and lime. They make all the sauces and salsas fresh every day.

Moon Time (Pub food from Culinary Institute)
1602 E. Sherman Ave.
Coeur d'Alene, ID 83814
208-667-2331

Moon Time is an English-style pub with a great selection of beers on tap as well as a decent array of wine. The food is a step above traditional Pub Grub. Try the rosemary infused Lamb burger, or the 74th St. gumbo. (The daily specials are always a good bet as well.)

The Gewurztraminer grape dates back to the Middle Ages in the form of its parent variety, traminer. As the grape mutated over the centuries one was prized above all the others, a dark pinkish-brown, spotted berry with an amazing perfumed aroma. The Alsatians called it gewürztraminer but it wasn't until 1973 that the name was officially sanctioned. A 375 ml bottle of Karthauser Gewurztraminer Trockenberenauslese goes for $300.00 but we believe if you can pronounce it you should get a discount.

Syringa Café (Japanese/Sushi)
1401 N. Fourth St.
Coeur d'Alene, ID 83814
208-664-2718

Syringa is one of four sushi restaurants in Coeur d'Alene. While North Idaho may seem like an odd place for sushi remember that the Spokane airport is just 45 minute drive away and has flights to Seattle every hour. Named for the state flower of Idaho, Syringa is overseen by Chef Viljo and wife Autumn. Arguably the best sushi in the area and rivaling anything Seattle has to offer. Viljo's resume includes several years under Chef Thierry Rautureau in the kitchen at Seattle's venerable French restaurant, Rovers. (While you are in the area you can walk across the street to **Pilgrim's Natural Foods**. (You might even see one of the authors working there or at least see Dave trying to find out if he is in the back room). Coeur d'Alene's only Natural Food Market also features one of the area's best wine and beer selections.

Tony's on the Lake (Italian)
6823 E. Coeur d'Alene Lake Dr.
Coeur d'Alene, ID 83814
208-667-9885

This dining institution on Coeur d'Alene Lake has re-opened under the guidance of Chef Cheyenne D'Alessandro. Her parents, Paul and Bonnie, are grandchildren of Tuscan immigrants who came to the states in 1909. Cheyenne graduated from the Culinary Institute of America in Hyde Park, New York and also studied in Florence. The gourmet Italian cuisine and lake view make this place worth the drive to experience a summer evening in the Northwest.

Taco Truck (On the move Mexican)

One half block east of
Appleway and Fourth Street

Wine Cellar (Bistro with local musicians)
313 E. Sherman Ave.
Coeur d'Alene, ID 83814
208-664-9463

For a lively scene we like the Wine Cellar in downtown Coeur d'Alene. The combination of reliably good food, a well thought out wine list and live blues has made this a favorite of local diners. A new addition is the sidewalk Tapas bar. One of the best bargains in town is the Italian three course dinner. You get a choice of pasta for your first course (including house-made gnocchi or puttanesca) an entrée (such as lamb Osso buco, chicken stuffed with chevre or bouillabaisse) and a salad or dessert. All this for $17.

White House Grill (Mediterranean)
620 N. Spokane St.
Post Falls, ID 83854
208-777-9672

If you find yourself in Post Falls you are most likely lost, but why not make the most of it by stopping in at Whitehouse Grill. This Mediterranean place offers a fun, casual atmosphere, lots of garlic, and a chance to be entertained by Raci, the slightly crazy owner. While you are there, stroll next door to Enoteca, a good wine shop with a great beer selection.

Wolf Lodge Inn (Steak)
11741 E Frontage Rd.
Exit 22
Eight Miles East of CDA
Coeur d'Alene, ID 83814
208-664-6665

For a bit of North Idaho "ambiance" Wolf Lodge serves up big steaks (aged on-site and cooked over an open fire) with baked beans, Indian fry-bread, and no white tablecloths. Cowboy hats are appropriate, but not required.

Coffee

Bakery by the Lake
314 N. Third St.
Coeur d'Alene, ID 83814
208-415-0681

Bella Rose
213 E Sherman Street
Coeur d'Alene, ID 83814
208-667-9640

Calypso Coffee
116 E. Lakeside Ave.
Coeur d'Alene, ID 83814
208-665-0591

Java on Sherman
324 Sherman Ave.
Coeur d'Alene, ID 83814
208-667-0010

Breakfast

Franklin's Hoagies (breakfast and lunch)
501 N. Fourth St.
Coeur d'Alene, ID 83814
208-664-3998

Michael D's Eatery
203 Coeur d'Alene Lake Dr.
Coeur d'Alene, ID 83814
208-676-9049

The Pinot Gris grape is a mutant of the Pinot Noir grape. In 1966 David Lett of Oregon's Eyrie Vineyards planted the first Pinot Gris grapes in the Northwest. Hubert Trimbach (Alsace, France) told me that Pinot Gris was given to mankind so we could drink it while eating salmon. (This grape dates back to at least 1375 when Cistercian Monks planted the grapes in Badacsony, Hungary. Those monks seem to like their grapes.)

Pubs

Capones Sports Pub (More taps than tables)
751 N. Fourth St.
Coeur d'Alene, ID 83814
208-667-4843

Parkside Bistro & Pub (Pub next to City Park)
414 Mullan Rd.
Coeur d'Alene, ID 83814
208-765-8220

Malbec in free fall

The Malbec grape is one of six grapes approved for making red wines in the Bordeaux region of France. (The approved grapes for blending in Bordeaux are: Merlot, Cabernet Sauvignon, Cabernet Franc, Malbec, Petit Verdot and Grand Vidure.)

Malbec is reported to go by four hundred different names which is one of the reasons that the wine's popularity has declined over the years. (Pressac or Cot or Auxerrois in France; Tinta Amarela in Portugal and Portugal Malbec in Australia). It is mainly used to add color and tannin to wines. Malbecs from Argentina seem to thrive where hot summer temperatures and a long growing season allow the grape to ripen and soften its tannins.

Part VIII –

Gotta Eat

Lewiston to Sandpoint

Pullman/Moscow

We would be remiss if we didn't mention the Moscow Wine Company which has been supportive of the Washington and Idaho wine industry since the early 1980s. The Moscow Wine Company in Moscow, Idaho has been bringing in wines from all over the world for more than twenty-five years. Terry and Dennis have been educating people in wine, cheese and gourmet food items long before it was fashionable to do so in the northwest, let alone Moscow, Idaho.

Swilly's
200 NE. Kamiaken
Pullman, WA
509-334-3395

Chef Joan Swensen has been serving food at Swilly's since 1995. The food is a Palouse version of San Francisco fusion. One of the gems in the wheat country. Swilly's is worth scheduling lunch or dinner at while you are visiting the wineries or Washington State University.

Nectar Restaurant
105 W. Sixth St.
Moscow, ID 83843
208-882-5914

A relative newcomer to the area Nectar offers seasonal cuisine. Their beef comes from a local farm, Eaton's Ranch, and they use local produce in season. They have an extensive wine list with emphasis on wines from Washington and Oregon.

Red Door
215 S. Main
Moscow, ID 83843
208-882-7830

The Red Door was one of the first restaurants in the area to use the slow cook revolution as part of their cooking repertoire. You can get house cured salmon, spicy fire cracker balls of yellow fin tuna, duck breast prosciutto, wild Alaskan halibut, slow cooked wild boar shoulder, bison short ribs to name a few of their ever changing menu items. A good wine list and don't forget dessert.

West of Paris (French)
403 S. Main St.
Moscow, ID 83842
208-596-8189

French cuisine prepared with fresh local ingredients and a limited, but well thought out wine list.

Lewiston/Clarkston

Starbucks (coffee)
1325 21st
Lewiston, ID 83501
208-798-0627

Sycamore Street Grill
900 Sixth St.
Clarkston, WA 99403
509-751-0881

For many years I just passed through the Lewiston/Clarkston area figuring that the last good meal was when Sacagawea fried fresh fish up for the boys from Missouri. If I did stop I was resigned to burgers, grilled tuna fish sandwiches (ahi is more of a formal greeting than a fish here) and a bowl of barley soup. Sycamore's changed my mind and I would make it a point to plan my trip through this area around dinner time. They have a good selection of Italian food as well as steaks and seafood.

Sandpoint

Coffee

Heavenly Latte
120 Cedar
Sandpoint, ID 83864
208-265-4376

Monarch Mountain Coffee
208 N. Fourth Ave.
Sandpoint, ID 83864
208-265-9382

Restaurants

Arlos Ristorante (Italian)
330 N. First Ave.
Sandpoint, ID 83864
208-255-4186

Bangkok Cuisine (Thai)
202 N Second St.
Sandpoint, ID 83864
208-265-4149

The Cabernet Franc grape is one of the principal red grape varietals in the Loire Valley of France and can be a main component of the Bordeaux commune wines of St. Emilion in Bordeaux. (Most notably Cheval Blanc—a single 750 ml bottle of the 1947 Cheval Blanc has gone for $15,6000.00. I imagine that Anton Ego, food critic in *Ratatouille*, was on an expense account.) In the late 1990s Dr. Meredith of University of California, Davis, determined through DNA testing that it was one of the parents of the Cabernet Sauvignon grape.

Café Trinity (Modern American)
116 N. First Ave.
Sandpoint, ID 83864
208-255-7558

Eichardt's Pub, Grill and Coffee House
212 Cedar St.
Sandpoint, ID 83864
208-263-4005

Hydra Restaurant (Continental since 1975)
115 Lake St.
Sandpoint, ID 83864
208-263-7123

Ivano's Ristorante (Italian)
124 S. Second St.
Sandpoint, ID 83864
208-263-0211

Alexei – self portrait

Part IX

GOTTA SLEEP

(Coeur d'Alene)

Ameritel Inn
333 Ironwood Drive
Coeur d'Alene, Idaho 83814
208-665-9000

Best Western Inn
506 W. Appleway
Coeur d'Alene, Idaho 83814
208-765-3200

Coeur d'Alene Resort
115 S. Second Ave.
Coeur d'Alene, ID 83846
208-765-4000

La Quinta Inn
280 E. Appleway
Coeur d'Alene, Idaho 83814
208-664-0433

Resort City Inn
621 E. Sherman Ave.
Coeur d'Alene, Idaho 83814
208-676-1225

(Pullman/Moscow)

Best Western University Inn
1516 W Pullman Rd
Moscow, ID 83843
208-882-0550

Quality Inn Paradise Creek
1400 SE Bishop Blvd.
Pullman, WA 99163
509-332-0500

(Sandpoint, Idaho)

Best Western-Edgewater Resort
56 Bridge St.
Sandpoint, ID 83864
208-263-9581

Lodge at Sandpoint
41 Lakeshore Dr.
Sagle, ID 83860
208-263-2211

Schweitzer Mountain Resort
10000 Schweitzer Mountain Rd.
Sandpoint, ID 83864
208-263-9555

Charles Dickens wrote about hotel views in *The Uncommercial Traveller – Travelling Abroad.* "At Paris, I took an upper apartment for a few days in one of the hotels of the Rue de Rivoli; my front windows looking into the garden of the Tuileries (where the principal difference between the nursemaids and the flowers seemed to be that the former were locomotive and the latter not .." I bring this up because Sam says he saw Tulips running through a field of maidens on his last trip to Sandpoint so beware of where you stay.

Part X

Spokane & Coeur d'Alene Links

www.coeurdalene.com

www.cdachamber.com

www.spokanecity.org

www.spokane.net

www.spokaneoutdoors.com

www.spokanearts.com

Charles Dickens wrote about reading travel books in *The Long Voyage*. You might want to contemplate these thoughts while you are going through this book with a critic's sword, wondering how you might one day meet the authors and inflict the same pleasure on them that you have derived from reading this tome.

"When the wind is blowing and the sleet or rain is driving against the dark windows, I love to sit by the fire, thinking of what I have read in books of voyage and travel."

We hope you have the same feeling reading about our travels and of course, sip a glass of Walla Walla Valley, Spokane or Northern Idaho wine while you are so doing.

In Conclusion:

We know that this book's information will always be changing. We hope you have enjoyed part of the journey with us; the rest of the journey is up to you. Let us know when something should be added to the cemetery, when addresses or phone numbers need to be corrected or changed and let us know when you find a hidden gem – that's what this journey is all about.

Send information to:

Dave Westfall, 906 W. Second Ave., Spokane, WA 99201

Dave Westfall grew up in Spokane, Washington and attended North Central High School. Upon graduation he went to Harvard University and after completion of his degree he was awarded a Rockefeller Scholarship to Tanzania in 1972-1973. He then attended the University of British Columbia in Vancouver, British Columbia before returning to Spokane and pursuing a wine career. Dave has been a caterer, a manager of a retail wine shop; he started a fine wine distributorship before opening Grande Ronde Cellars in 1997.

Sam Lange grew up in Spokane, Washington and attended Shadle Park High School (and he still has his marching band kilts to this day). Sam then went to the University of Idaho and opened a rival retail wine shop to Dave's in 1984. For eighteen years Sam was the wine buyer at the Coeur d'Alene Resort and garnered many honors including the Grand Award Winner from Wine Spectator. Sam is currently writing articles and books about wine and overseeing the Pilgrim's wine program.

Cheers, Dave and Sam

Glossary

AVA American Viticultural Area – An area that has been recognized by the federal government for a distinctive combination of soil, climate and topography which contributes to the identifiable regional character of the wine.

Biodynamic "Biodynamics is a holistic farming approach developed in the 1920s by the Austrian scientist-philosopher Rudolf Steiner. While it encompasses many of the principles of organic farming, such as the elimination of all synthetic chemicals, Biodynamics goes further, requiring close attention to the varied forces of nature influencing the vine. It also emphasized a closed, self-sustaining ecosystem." (From the Benziger site www.benziger.) Go to this site to read more about the relationships between crop fertility, balance of the animal population, how increased nutrients in the soil adds to the character of wine, etc. The Demeter Association is another source for information on this type of farming (www.demeterbta.com).

Organic This method of farming avoids synthetic chemicals. The farming methods include crop rotation, natural composts as well as natural methods to control weeds, insects and other pests (including wine tasters).

VINEA Voluntary group of Walla Walla Valley winegrowers that have embraced a covenant with environmental, economic and social sustainability concurrent with their production of grapes and wines.